World Work

A Lorian Textbook

Other books by
David Spangler

Blessing: *The Art and the Practice*

The Call

Parent as Mystic - Mystic as Parent

Manifestation: *Creating the life you love*

The Story Tree

Lorian Textbook Series

Incarnational Spirituality

Starshaman Home Mystery School™

- *Home-Crafting: Self, Sacred and Blessing*
- *Space-Crafting: The Incarnational Self*
- *Crafting Inner Alliances: Working with*
  Spiritual Forces*
- *World-Crafting: Manifestation and Service**

* In Progress

World Work

This Lorian Textbook is the transcript of an online class called *World Work?* It has minimal editing to preserve the flavor of the original class. The content has been shaped in part by the unique nature of the class itself.

David Spangler

World Work

Edited by Jeremy Berg

Cover Art by Deva Berg

Published by Lorian Press
2204 E Grand Ave.
Everett, WA 98201

ISBN: 0-936878-15-0
978-0-936878-15-7

Spangler/David
World Work/David Spangler

Printed in the United States of America

0 9 8 7 6 5 4 3 2 1

www.lorian.org

Dedication

The material in this book has been adapted from an online class offered by the Lorian Association in 2003 and taught by David Spangler. It is to those original class participants and to all who join this class that this textbook is dedicated.

You will note that the current issues which are referenced and the examples date from the period in which the text was written. It was not originally written to be presented in a linear way as necessitated by this printed format. An online classroom environment allows for moving back and forth along several lines of conversation and engagement simultaneously. In addition the language is somewhat more conversational than you might expect in a book as the David knew all of the people participating in the class personally. However, we feel that there is value in what is presented here and an attempt has been made to create an order of presentation that is reasonably easy to follow. We hope you enjoy it and the ideas and exercises presented here. We hope they can become a help to you in your participation in the great work.

Contents

Chapter One
Introduction to Incarnational Spirituality

Incarnational Spirituality is the art and practice of evoking and using inner resources of energy arising from the act of incarnation itself order to shape one's life, bless one's world, and become a partner with the creative forces of spirit. Parts of this approach may seem familiar to you and other parts may seem new. Most of the material that makes up this approach comes out of my intuitive and clairvoyant research sustained over many years of interaction with subtle, supersensory, non-physical beings and realms. Arising from a partnership with spiritual worlds does not give this material any special authority as "revelation," or any special, infallible authenticity. Like the fruits of any research, the insights that make up Incarnational Spirituality need to be tested in an individual's life to determine their usefulness or accuracy for that individual. Without such testing, they remain hypotheses.

The research of Incarnational Spirituality is ongoing and a work-in-progress. I and the faculty and students of Lorian have been testing and living this spirituality for years with positive effects and are confident of its value to add meaning to a person's life and service to the world. Using Incarnational Spirituality as our foundation and philosophy, we have been teaching classes ranging from one-day workshops to our year long programs and have seen the benefits people have received from this approach.

A strategy to bless our World
~ Three Levels of Change ~

Incarnational Spirituality is more than a personal spiritual practice for inner development or private attunement. It is also a way of giving service and of enhancing our capacities to serve. It is a way of bringing change into our world, beginning with ourselves. There are three levels of change that Incarnational Spirituality explores:

1

1. Inner Change: This is the change we can make in our personal Self. These are changes of worldview, attitude, orientation, and energy. A central element of Incarnational Spirituality is the shift we can make within ourselves that opens us to the generative power and energy of our own incarnational spirit.

2. Individual Life Change: This is the change we can bring to the shape of our lives and to our immediate relationships and environment. Two examples of this are the arts of manifestation and blessing.

3. World Work or Change in the World: Using the resources of our incarnational spirit, we add our energies to the inner and outer forces of change in the world.

Incarnational Spirituality arises from these basic premises:

1. The act of incarnation is the primal act from that creation that emerges from the Generative Mystery of the Sacred. The cosmos is the incarnation of the Sacred.

2. Our individual acts of incarnation are a fractal or resonant expression of this primal sacred act, a means by which we participate in and manifest sacredness ourselves.

3. Incarnation is more than a singular event, i.e., the means by which we become physical individuals through birth into this world. Incarnational Spirituality is a process that is ongoing.

4. The act of incarnation generates creative energy. Consequently, our act of incarnating into this world released a burst of spiritual and vital energy that is part of who we are. It is an inner resource upon which we can draw.

5. At the heart of the incarnational process is a generative source that is the essence of Self, our sacred individuality and sovereignty. This Sovereignty is present and can be tapped within all manifestations of Self, from the mystery and depths of the Soul to the everyday

expressions of the personality.

6. An objective of Incarnational Spirituality is to understand and inhabit all levels of Self with love and honor as a means of unfolding the coherency and power of our unique spiritual Presence as a blessing in the world.

7. Incarnation is an act of resonance between the individual and the universal. Incarnational Spirituality calls us to use our own incarnational process and sovereignty to partner with, participate in, and enhance the universal and sacred spirit of Incarnation itself, in honor, blessing, and empowerment for all the other acts of incarnation that make up our world.

Where do these premises come from?

Here's a personal story. When I first began my public work as a teacher in 1965, I entered into a partnership with a non-physical being whom I called "John." I could see and communicate with this being through the use of senses operating beyond the range of our normal physical senses. I have always been able to do this to some degree my entire life. As a child, I thought the inner worlds were simply a normal part of the world as a whole. John was a friend, partner, and mentor who helped me sharpen and discipline my inner senses so that they became more effective tools in doing the spiritual research and investigation that has been my particular calling in life.

One day early in our relationship, he said to me, "You do not simply receive spiritual energies from God or from transpersonal sources. You are yourself, as an incarnate individual, a source of spiritual energy. Human beings are not simply conduits for spiritual forces from higher levels to pass through you into the world; each person is a unique generative source of such forces in ways appropriate to the world in which you live." I confess this didn't mean much to me at the time, other than as an affirmation of the value and importance of each individual.

Some years later, I became aware, first with the people with whom I was working in classes and then subsequently with people whom I just met in the course of my everyday activities, that there was a subtle energy around them that seemed new to me. It was an inner phenomenon I didn't recognize. It was a spiritual energy that was akin to the kind of energies that came from higher, non-physical levels, but it did not seem to be coming from that realm so as far as I could determine. Investigating this, I discovered that it did not come from a transpersonal aspect of the individual but was emerging from the inner dynamics of the personal life. The incarnate life as individuals engaged with their world was not an emotional or mental energy but a spiritual force capable of empowerment and blessing the same as any spiritual force originating in the higher realms. I called this force the "empersonal spirit," meaning that it was arising from or emerging out of the personal dimension of our lives, rather than, say, the transpersonal. It became a key element in how I taught the art of blessing, as described in my book of that name.

As I continued to explore and work with this energy, my perceptions went deeper. I realized that this energy initially emerged from the act of incarnating into the physical realm. It was as if we crossed a boundary when coming into this world and in doing so triggered a release of energy from the spirit of the world itself that then became part of our own individual pattern. I discovered that this empersonal spirit was not the whole picture.

In investigating this empersonal spirit, I recalled something John had said some years before. I found myself touching a generative source of Light and spiritual energy within the life of each person. This source was not quite the same thing as the "sacred within" or the soul or a "higher self," though as a spiritual energy it had obvious connections and resonance with all of these. What it seemed to be was the quality of "source-ness" or of being a generative source itself. It was intimately tied to the act and process of incarnation as a sacred activity. It was more than just the transference of one's consciousness from one realm to another. It was in further exploring this quality of being a source and the process of incarnation itself that a number of insights and hypotheses arose, some of which are expressed in the premises I listed above, and all of which constitute the developing and emerging art of Incarnational Spirituality.

4

Incarnation

Since we're talking about an Incarnational Spirituality, how do I define "incarnation"? Let me start with a metaphor. Imagine an actor stepping onto a stage to participate in a play. As soon as she does so, she is in the play. But merely being onstage is not enough. She now needs to engage with and respond to the other actors on the stage, to the story that is unfolding, and to the audience who is watching.

There is more to being in a play than simply being present and onstage! A step to that engagement is to be aware of all the elements that are present that make up the production. These elements include the actor's own talents, past experience, knowledge of his or her lines, knowledge of the play, awareness of the audience and their needs, awareness of the other actors, and awareness of the props and set that are present on stage. The actor must connect to what is present through knowledge, instinct, craft, and senses. A failure to do so, such as ignorance of the placement of props on the set, can lead to an actor stumbling over something. A disconnection from the script can lead to an actor missing his cue or fumbling her lines.

Connection also means that the actor is in the right play. It means that she has not studied and practiced to be part of Hamlet and now discovers herself on the stage of Romeo and Juliet. It means she has what it takes to be connected to the play she is in. An actor can also be onstage and connected and engage in a limited way. By fulfilling the role he has been given, saying his lines when appropriate, moving about the stage as appropriate, speaking loudly enough to be heard, and so forth, he is doing his job. But in this case, he is not really a master of his craft. He doesn't bring something extra to the production, something uniquely his own. He is just doing what he is told to do in order to be part of the play and gets a paycheck.

An actor who really knows her craft, who reaches out to the other actors and enables them to shine and fulfill their roles more effectively, and who embraces the audience has charisma and presence. Such an actor, who brings herself into the role and gives it that added dimension of drama and reality, texture and presence, is someone who brings the whole event alive. She creates a wholeness in which fellow actors, the story, the audience, and the stage are all uplifted. Then the production achieves a level of coherency and wholeness that makes it more than just a play or an evening's entertainment. It becomes a deep experience. Something emerges that is more than just the story or the sets or the actors or the audience. I know I've had experiences in the theater when that has happened, and it has been remarkable. I've also seen productions where the actors are wooden and just going through the motions of the play, speaking the lines of dialog but not infusing any life or craft into the narrative. Boring!

One might describe the process here as:

• Being (one's presence on the stage - Embodiment),

• Connecting (being aware of the other actors, the props, the set, the audience, one's own training as an actor, etc.),

• Engaging (participating in the drama, interacting with the other actors, the set, the audience, bringing one's craft into play, etc.),

• Emergence (the overall gestalt of the play, the quality of the production, the energy that's generated and released for all involved.

Incarnation is usually seen as synonymous with Embodiment. To incarnate is to take on a body that enables you to be part of the realm in which you are incarnating. Certainly that is part of it, but it is not all of it, anymore than just being on stage is equivalent to taking part in the play. Just "Being" is not enough to be incarnated. More is required. Connection, Engagement, and Emergence represent that something extra. Incarnation, then, is a synthesis of Being, Connection, Engagement, and Emergence.

Being born puts us on the stage of this world. It gives us a body. Usually this is what is meant by incarnation. After all, the literal meaning of the word is "into flesh" or "into meat." But incarnation, in the context of Incarnational Spirituality, is much more than that, and in a broad sense, neither begins nor ends with our physical birth or our physical death. What I call the "incarnational round" includes a pre-birth state and a post-mortem state. That is a topic for another time

Even if we measure incarnation from physical birth to physical death, merely being in a physical body is only a part of incarnation. Equally important are the qualities of connection, engagement, and emergence. Incarnation is a process of connection, engagement, and emergence with the world. Like participating in a play, it is something we are doing all the time, not something that happened once when we entered on stage, with everything following being merely the working out of that initiating event. Furthermore, incarnation is creativity at work. It is a creative process and part of the larger creative process from which humanity, society, the earth, and the cosmos emerge.

When we participate in incarnation, we participate in our own unique way in the process by which all that is comes into being. One of the images that I use to symbolize incarnation is that of a chalice or cup. I think of incarnation as essentially a sacred act and I often image it as a grail. This is because a cup is a marriage of boundary and space, the finite and the infinite, both of which are necessary to manifest an identity in the form of a specific "domain of activity." Hold a cup in your hand and you can see this quite clearly.

The body of the cup, the rim, the container, is a specific boundary; it encloses a specific space, which is the volume of the cup. Put your finger inside the cup and wiggle it, then take your finger out and wiggle it in the air. It's the same space. Space is Space. But if I pour my coffee into the air, it will spill and splatter all over the place. The space in the air will not hold the coffee so I can drink it. If I pour the coffee into the cup, though, then the space will fill with coffee that is held and contained so that I can lift it to my lips and drink it.

With a boundary, (or a membrane, a definition, a limit, an edge), we define a space and give it an identity, which is often an identity of function. We give it the capacity to hold. What it holds depends on the specific nature of the boundary and the nature of our intent. What do we want it to hold?

Notes & Reflections

Section One

Chapter Two:
Introduction to World Work

World Work is my term for our inner engagement with the world using our subtle energies and our spirit. I will probably need to come up with another term, since I don't want this to be confused with psychologist's Arnold Mindell's excellent concept of "World Work" which involves programs of face-to-face conflict resolution and psychological healing. But I'll use it for the moment. After all, the world can probably use all kinds of work!

World work may be focused upon specific events or situations in the world, such as the current diplomatic and potentially military conflict with Iraq, but it actually encompasses much more. As we shall explore, world work is as much about who we are in the world as about what we do or how we do it.

In its simplest form, world work is the flow of compassion and a restorative, balancing resource from me to my world. I might do this through prayer, meditation, ritual, inner participation and presence, or the projection of Light or energy from my personhood to another or to a situation. Compassion links me through love with the object of my concern. The "restorative, balancing resource" simply means that the essence of what I want to have happen is for a condition of wholeness, connectedness, balance, love, flow, and attunement to be restored in that person or in that situation.

I may not know until I actually begin the work itself just what that resource might be. It could be love, it could be a healing energy, it could be insight, it could be a warrior force, it could be any number of qualities or manifestations of energy. It is whatever the situation needs and whatever I am able to offer that will restore wellbeing, harmony, and balance.

I think of it this way. There is hunger in the world, but not everyone can eat the same food, nor do I always know just what food may best fit a need. So my task is to cultivate a rich garden as well as to develop means of distribution. However, and this is very important, I'm not the only gardener. Others are growing food as well, so I don't have to produce everything. The world does not need to be fed from my garden alone. My task is to cultivate a garden that is as abundant as possible in harmony with the nature of the terrain and the soil that I currently have to work with.

I can "burn out" my garden if I try to grow too much, or if I overgrow and do not allow for periods of lying fallow and letting the soil regenerate. Likewise, if I try to grow things that belong in different soil or in different conditions than my garden can offer, I can end up with plants that are not as healthy as they might otherwise be.

So in approaching world work, I need to understand that I have rich inner resources that I can cultivate and develop with which to grace my world, but the world is not dependent on me alone, nor can I do everything that is needed. To transmit balance and harmony, I need to experience balance and harmony in my own life.

This does not mean that we have to be perfect before we can engage in world work. Far from it! We need not be spiritual masters in order to be spiritual collaborators with the World Soul and the wellbeing of all life everywhere. It just means that part of world work is the cultivation of our inner resources, those qualities that we would offer to our world. It is a work of learning and practicing qualities of love, forgiveness, grace, joy, blessing, wholeness, balance, humor, power, courage, gratefulness, appreciation, and so forth.

Sometimes, I observe that we think of these qualities in BIG ways, as if they represent tremendous feats of spiritual athleticism. But they are actually ordinary qualities that we experience everyday. They are within the range of normal human activity and experience, just like walking and breathing are not things that only trained athletes can do.

To practice loving the world can mean something as simple as being more mindful of the ordinary things in my life and the ordinary actions I do everyday and discovering how to love them or use them as channels for my love. It can mean something as simple as expanding my heart a little bit each day to love something new or something that the day before I did not love or perhaps didn't even notice. It need not mean that I must engulf the whole world in my love in one huge gulp!

I think of World Work as having the following aspects:

1. Cultivation of those qualities that bring blessing, fostering, harmony, love, and grace into my everyday life and world.

2. Mindful engagement with the ordinary "stuff" in my everyday life and world such that each engagement becomes an opportunity to practice and cultivate these qualities.

3. The focused use of my inner resources and qualities in a mindful engagement with a particular situation.

In this text we will primarily be looking at this third aspect because the first two constitute a living spiritual practice that encompasses our whole lives and is beyond the scope of just this textbook alone. But the first two aspects will always be present as background to our work, and I shall certainly return to them as we go along when necessary.

Another way to look at World Work is to say that it is engagement with the mystery of the Earth, just as healing is an engagement with the mystery of the body and soul. Of course, much of medicine and healing is based on well-known information such as anatomy, physiology, and the like. But the power of the body to heal itself and restore its wholeness even when medical science would say such restoration is impossible is well-documented. For all our knowledge, the body and its interaction with mind, emotion and soul remains mysterious—or perhaps I should say beyond the usual boundaries of what the rational, materialistic mind claims as reality.

Doing world work is similar. Though we may focus our attention upon a particular issue or situation, the way a doctor or healer focuses upon a particular wound or illness, we are still engaging with deep and powerful forces within the body of the earth and humanity, the world soul, and the human soul. We are dealing with Mystery.

We approach Mystery with humility and openness. We may think we know what a situation is all about and what it demands, but our knowledge may well be incomplete. We need to be informed—formed— by Mystery in a way that our will and intent collaborate gracefully with it.

So part of World Work is the will to serve, to help, to bless, to bring healing, and so forth, but part of it is the will to listen, to attune, to be informed.

There are many questions involved in this kind of work and some discussion of the underlying cosmology as I see it may be helpful. Does anything I do subjectively, such as prayer or visualization, really have an effect somewhere else separated from me in space and time? If I am sending "energy," let us say, to Afghanistan, what actually is going on? If a force does emerge from me in some fashion, how is it transmitted? What kind of force is it? Is there a beam of some nature traveling from me across the Atlantic, across Europe and into central Asia where it does something with somebody? Is it like a radio wave or a lightning bolt? Can it be interfered with?

I don't pretend to know the answer to those questions in any objectively scientific way. I have no idea how one would set up a proper scientific experiment to determine these answers. On the other hand, there is some interesting scientific research being done in this area of global consciousness and connectedness.

What is important is that we approach this work with a degree of humility which gives us a freedom from the words and concepts, like "consciousness," "energy," "spirit," and so forth which while useful may not truly represent or communicate just what is going on or the forces and phenomena involved. In other words, when we try to be too descriptive and cosmological about this process (i.e., "I am affecting global consciousness through the transmission of my spiritual energy across the astral plane into the etheric web and along lines of force and polarity to fill the situation with light."), we can end up putting ourselves into a cognitive straight-jacket.

The interesting thing is that I don't have to understand or explain what is going on in order for it to work, just as I don't have to know what my computer is doing in order for me to write and then post this material. There is more than ample evidence that prayer works, but does it work because it is a communication with God who then does what I ask, or because it set energy into motion, or for some other reason? We may all have opinions about this, but when prayer works, research has shown it does so independently of any particular methodology.

In my own experience, what is important is a certain quality and depth of engagement. There does seem to me to be a threshold (perhaps more than one) involved, and if I cross that threshold, whatever methodology I use, I can have an effect. If I don't, I won't. This effect may be direct or it may be indirect, setting up a cascade of effects like rolling a small stone down a hill can produce an avalanche of stones.

So in our work here together we are going to explore just what this threshold may be and how we can cross it.

Part of the crossing of this threshold, it seems to me, is through the use of imagination. Imagination is more than just the creation of imagery. It is an act of organization and connection. That is, the act of imagining is like injecting a grain of sand into an oyster around which a pearl will develop. The power of any imaginative image is related to the size of pearl that it can produce within the oyster of consciousness. We'll explore this more later, but I would suggest here that the questions of methodology and cosmology such as I raised above fall into this category of imagination. That is, how I imagine world work or prayer works is important not as a description of what is happening but as a way of deepening my imaginative engagement: the "oystering" of the grain of sand.

A second aspect to crossing this threshold lies with our experience of individuality and our incarnational spirit, or what I have called our "empersonal" spirit. It is the quality of our uniqueness; more importantly, it is the quality of our "newness" or "freshness." It is the presence of ourselves as an on-going act of revelation. In each of us, God speaks as if for the first time. It is our personal embodiment of mystery. We'll explore this a bit more later, as well.

Another part of crossing this threshold is through what I call "presence." Presence to me is a synergistic, emergent phenomenon, arising co-creatively from the resources I bring and from my individuality and from the resources present in my inner and outer environments. It is a phenomenon of coherency: how coherent am I within myself, how coherent am I with my surroundings, how coherent am I with the object of my world work or prayer, how coherent am I with resources that I choose to invoke?

Coherency is not quite the same to me as wholeness. I think of wholeness as a condition, but I think of coherency as an activity, as something dynamic and in process, like my sense of balance as I walk across a tightrope. In that example, I am maintaining coherency between my body, the rope, the earth far below me, the space about me, and my intent to get from one end of the rope to the other. Coherency arises from engagement and action of some nature.

Also, we use the word to signify when something has meaning or makes sense, as in "He began to speak coherently." This conveys to me a condition of communication, which may be appropriate when thinking about world work for it could be seen as an act of communicating a spiritual intent into the world.

So in exploring world work, we are going to be exploring and working with individuality, imagination and coherency or presence as our primary tools. They are, in a sense, the essence of the cosmology that will guide us in this process.

World work allows us to participate in world affairs at a synchronistic level of connectedness and being. World work, like other forms of spiritual work, works at a level other than the normal everyday world of physical objects, space and time. Different cosmologies define that level (or levels) in different ways. Thus we have concepts like "astral plane," "etheric plane," "etheric web," "planetary consciousness," and the like. These can be very useful concepts, just as the idea of "energy" can be useful in our imaginative descriptions.

When I do world work, however, I rarely experience anything like what is usually meant by these terms. I don't act from an astral or etheric level, as far as I can tell, and I don't send out energies of any kind. What I do experience is entering into a relationship with a condition that might simply be called "the place where synchronicity happens." But this is not just a psychological space; it feels to me to have real dimensionality. It is as if I discover in myself the metaphysical cognates of conditions, places or people in the physical world. This would be like the "Afghanistan within," or the "White House within" or "Osama bin Laden within." I find myself in touch with something—a presence perhaps—that represents in this place of working its counterpart in the physical world.

This sounds a bit like traditional magic: working with correspondences. It conjures up images like sticking pins in a voodoo doll or using fire to represent divine light. But it is not as simple and one-to-one as that. It is more like working on the whole world at once

15

in order to affect a part of it, because nothing exists independently but all things exist in interconnection. In this sense, it is more like an image of holistic healing in which to affect one part of the body, the practitioner works on a number of seemingly unrelated other parts in order to restore the whole body to coherency and wholeness. To use an example from current news, it is not so much that I send Light to Afghanistan as that I use Afghanistan as a way of engaging with the wholeness of the world to adjust it towards a healthier state.

So world work to me is not just sending light or goodwill or loving energy to some part of the globe that is in difficulty; it is a process of working on the whole world at once. It is engaging with an organic system, of which I am a part. And my power to affect this system arises in large measure precisely because I am a part of it. So part of world work to me is working on my part of being-the-world, my incarnational slice, in order to stimulate and affect the whole.

If working on the whole world at once seems like an immense affair, think of the trimtab, the device that allows a large ocean liner to steer. The force of the water against the rudder would ordinarily make it very hard to turn, but the trimtab, which is a very much smaller rudder, built onto the larger one, can turn more easily because of its size. When it turns, it changes the flow of water and hydraulic pressure around the large rudder that in turn enables the large rudder to turn more easily and hence turn the ship.

It is the principle of what is now being called "Ultra-high dilution biology," or the study of homeopathy in which an extremely dilute potion of something can have a large cascading effect within the body as a whole. It is, it seems to me, this kind of phenomenon with which we may be working when we do inner work, for we are in ourselves an ultra-high dilution of the world itself!

Well, enough of all this cosmology and speculating. It is time to get into some exercises and steps.

Notes & Reflections

The Exercises

This textbook includes exploratory exercises that constitute the practice (or "lab") side of the material and serve to illustrate the topic. Please try the exercise more than one time and record your experiences from each practice session in the space provided or in your personal journal. In Lorian's programs, much of the students' work revolves around doing exercises. Some of these exercises are like simple, mini-rituals; others are more reflective or contemplative. Some are intended to stimulate a particular kind of energy field around or within you, or connect you energetically with the world in a specific way. All are concerned with creating a state of mind and a felt sense within you.

An important element in doing these practices is a regular process for entering and leaving the state of mind that I metaphorically name "The Empty Stage". This exercise can be found on the following pages. Within this process, you can do all the exercises I am proposing in this text. Consistency is a huge help in this kind of work. It builds coherency into what you do.

Beyond that, the exercises I offer are just suggestions. They are not cast in concrete. If you understand the purpose of the exercise, then you can feel free to redesign it and adapt it to your particular style and needs. Indeed, I encourage you to do so, so that you can enjoy the exercise as your own. An exercise is a living thing, filled with spirit, and it should blend with you in a way that honors and fosters your own spirit. In doing the exercise, it should emerge from you as much as from me and transform itself in any way that is needful in order for that to happen. It may contain elements that you may not wish to do or that seem too elaborate or just not your "style." All I ask is that you understand and honor the purpose behind the exercise and the spirit it is intended to embody. Then feel free to change it or adapt it, as you need.

To paraphrase Jesus, "You were not made for the exercises: the exercises are made to serve you."

Try each exercise at least once as presented, but please feel free after that to modify the form of the exercise to configure it to your unique needs and style. At the same time, be sure to retain the integrity of the basic objective and intent.

If at any time in doing an exercise, you feel any physical, mental, emotional, or psychic distress (this might feel like discomfort, tiredness, restlessness, or an intuitive sense of "No" about doing it or continuing to do it) stop immediately. Close the boundaries, ground yourself, and shift your attention and energies. You can change your attention completely by doing something physical to shift and change your energy. For example, do something fun that makes you laugh. This is an excellent way to change your energy.

Having to stop an exercise doesn't necessarily mean that you've come into contact with something dangerous or harmful. It is simply a sign that for some reason, that may or may not be evident, your energy in the moment is not or is no longer compatible with what you're doing. It may be a matter of timing, it may be that you are tired, or it may be that this exercise is not for you. As I said above, make the exercise your own. If need be, adjust it so you feel comfortable with it, or find a substitute.

In doing these exercises, the rule "no pain, no gain" most definitely does not apply!

Unless you have a strong inner sense not to do so, I would recommend trying the exercise one more time later. If the sense of disturbance or uneasiness continues, then clearly this exercise is not for you. Either change it or find some equivalent or simply skip it entirely.

Most of the exercises I suggest in this text have been used successfully by other people in the past. Some have emerged more recently from my work or have suggested by my own colleagues within the Inner Worlds.

Exercise One:
The Empty Stage

This is a generic practice for entering into a mild altered state and back again. It's highly adaptable. The main objective is to enter an open, evocative, imaginal space within which images and contacts may arise, and then to leave it again in an appropriate manner. Because I love theater, for me the image of an empty stage is very powerful and evocative. But you may find a different image more potent for you. Please feel free to experiment. It's the state of evocative receptivity we're after, not a particular setting or image.

Entering the theater with the empty stage is a form of shifting from everyday awareness into a particular kind of altered consciousness oriented to inner journeys and working with imaginal states. In essence, it is a more elaborate form of lighting a candle!

1. Take time to relax and quiet your mind, your feelings, and your body.

2. Imagine that there is a threshold in front of you. This can take any form you wish, but the most natural may be the form of a door or portal that you will step through as you cross the threshold. This door is closed at first. Open it. If you feel the need, you can imagine guardians or allies standing on either side, protecting the door and threshold and protecting you as well.

3. Cross over the threshold. If you wish and if it will make you feel safe, you can imagine a guardian or ally crossing over with you.

4. You enter a theater. It is the theater of your heart and mind, the place of your imagination. It is a place of daydreams, fantasies, visualizations, images, and stories. You are standing at the back of the theater. In front of you are rows of theater seats and an empty stage. Go forward and sit in one of the seats in any of the rows. Look around and be aware of the theater around you, hushed and expectant for what may appear on stage.

5. In front of you is an empty stage, an empty space. Feel the

evocative, creative power of this space. Anything can take shape there. Any story could be told on that stage, any characters or settings could manifest upon it. Feel its imaginative power. Feel the wonder and anticipation at what might appear on this empty stage, this open space of potential and invocation. Appreciate its possibilities.

6. If you are doing an imaginative exercise, then it begins here at this step. Something appropriate to the exercise will appear on the stage and draw you into it. You will find yourself on the stage, the theater disappearing, and yourself immersed in the imaginal world of the exercise. When the exercise is complete, you will find yourself back on the stage, which is once again empty. You will again step down and find a seat in the audience where you will be energized, filled with grace and blessed.

7. Once you have a felt sense of this empty stage and its open, evocative, creative space, get up and go back out of the theater the way you came. Cross back through the door over the threshold into your everyday normal surroundings and your everyday, normal consciousness. Any guardians that went with you into the theater come back out and take up their posts by the door into the theater.

8. Give thanks for whatever you have received and for any allies or beings who assisted you. Give thanks to your inner theater of your heart and mind. Feel any energies that remain with you from being in the theater grounding themselves into your body if they feel positive or being released to the light and transformative power of your guardians or to the spirit of the sacred if they feel unsettling or negative. Feel the power of your own Light rising within you, gracefully integrating you back into the energies and fields of your daily life, but with full awareness of any blessings you have received from your experiences in the theater. As you feel comfortable and ready, go about your daily life.

Take some time to repeat this exercise, moving in and out of your theater, feeling the nature of that shift, and gaining a felt sense of the evocative, creative power of the empty stage. When you need to, you will be able to go directly to that felt sense and into that creative open space as a result of practicing this exercise.

Notes & Reflections

Exercise Two:
Reflections on World Work

Here is a reflective exercise to get us started.

This text is about doing "inner" or spiritual work for the world and for humanity as a whole (something I call "World Work"). There are many, many ways we can serve people and our earth in physical, political, economic, social, and environmental ways. But this text is about how we do so from our inner nature, from our souls—if you will—and from our hearts and minds. What is the nature of our inner actions which can complement or lead to outer actions?

So I would like you to think about your views on this and how you may already do this.

I would like you to think about what it means to you to do "inner' or spiritual, mystical, magical, prayerful, blessingful work for the earth and for humanity.

How do you currently go about this?

Do you have any particular technique or process?

Is it something you do regularly or just now and then when it seems appropriate, as when there is a world crisis?

What do you feel about the current state of the world and of humanity? (Don't be afraid to be optimistic!) Dig deeply for this one and don't just settle for surface feelings and thoughts stimulated by news reports...but don't neglect these surface feelings either. Do you feel we are in good shape, poor shape, going to Hell in a hand basket, on the verge of paradise, or muddling along as usual? How does it feel to you to be in the world at this time? Are you fearful, confident, happy, sad, etc. when you think about being in the world?

Are there any particular issues that are lively and up for you at the moment? (These do not have to be crises!)

Do you feel any particular inner connection with nature? With the earth? With humanity (other than being human, of course...)?

Does the idea of a "World Soul" have meaning for you? What do you think this might be?

In short, using these questions as guidelines, I'd like you to write a short piece describing how you already think about serving humanity and the world in an "inner" way and how you might go about doing this.

This reflective exercise will give us a sense of where we are starting from and what the current level of our experience in this area may be. Your writing need not be long, but I would like you to put some thought and reflection into it

Thank You!

Notes & Reflections

_____

_____

_____

_____

_____

_____

_____

_____

_____

_____

_____

_____

_____

_____

Chapter Three:
Standing

We begin our process with the simple act of standing.

A text imposes some artificiality upon our process.

The first is that I am going to divide the process of world work into steps. It will be easier for me to write about it that way. However, the work itself does not proceed in steps. It flows from your heart, mind, body and soul out into the world in an unbroken stream of compassion and will. Think of a dance performance. It is broken down by a choreographer into distinct pieces or movements which the dancers learn, but when it comes time to give the performance, all these pieces are melded together into one dance. World work is like that dance, but we will begin by looking at it as a series of movements or steps.

The second is that I am presenting it as a formal operation like a magical ritual. My assumption here is that you will take a moment of time during your day in which to focus and do "world work." But in actuality, world work is always proceeding, always unfolding from within you, for you are always in engagement with the world. You are part of the world, and that very fact makes whatever you do, think, feel, and say a form of world work. This is important because we can't just turn off our energy and prevent it from engaging with the world, however much we might like to. Whether we like it or not, we are always participating in the shaping of our world and the incarnation of the World Soul.

This is implicit in the very connectedness and fundamental unity that we invoke when explaining why magical or spiritual efforts have an effect. We assume that world work—spiritual work, inner work— works because we are all part of a great wholeness; we are all connected in some deep, synchronous fashion, part of an underlying order. But if this is true, then this is always true, not just when we want it to be true, not just when we are doing world work or some other kind of inner ritual or process. It is true when we are driving our cars, sitting at our desks, sitting on the toilet, climbing into bed, eating our dinner, watching our TV; whatever we are doing, it is true. Being true, something from us is always flowing into and along those lines or patterns or conditions of

26

connectedness—and something is always flowing back.

A major factor influencing this flow is our intentionality and our attentiveness, our will and our mindfulness. When I do world work in the sense that we are defining it in this text, I am putting effort and energy behind this connectedness; I am turning on the juice, turning up the volume, opening the valves. But the fact that I am always "on" to a certain degree, always connected, can also be used to our advantage and in fact, to my mind, is an integral part of the formal practice of world work itself in ways that we will see as we continue.

So let us continue!

The first step, the first movement in our dance, is "standing." Angeles Arrien calls this step "showing up." I sometimes refer to it as "being present." It is an attitude of being mindful and aware of oneself in the moment and within a particular environment. It is an attitude of attentiveness. It is the answer to the questions, "Where am I right now? Who am I right now?"

The simplest answer to these questions is the one given by our bodies. While minds and hearts can wander, bodies are always in the here and now. So I can look at where my feet are. I can look at what my eyes are seeing. I can feel what my fingers and toes can touch. I can smell what is in the air around me, hear what sounds are present and where they are coming from. I can feel the temperature.

When I just stand, all my moving parts have a chance to catch up with me. I go through my day scattering parts of me here and there, not physically of course (at least, I should hope not!), but a thought here, a feeling there, a concern someplace else. Parts of me move more slowly than other parts, they always seem to be playing catch up. But when I stop and just stand, everything has a chance to come to me. All my scattered images and thoughts and feelings can now nest in the branches of my attention, where before they could only fly about, never landing.

When I stand, I locate myself in time and space. My body, then my thoughts and feelings, say, "This is where I am. No place else. No when else. Just now. Just here." There is no ambiguity about this, a clarity, a concreteness that is refreshing. My body is not here in the living room and in the kitchen both, though my mind can be, trying to decide whether to eat or watch TV. Like the old Shaker song says, I have come down "where I ought to be." Which is, of course, just wherever I am.

This is a gift of the body to the soul. It locates me. It gives me solidarity. It gives me specificity. It relates me to time and space in a particular way. I am not smeared across the world in a state of unity, like an electron cloud forever trapped in its uncertainty principle. The probability wave has collapsed, and here I am. Right here. Right now. Just standing.

Standing is the recognition of a miracle. Have you ever considered the miracle of incarnation, that you are who you are and not someone else, that you are where you are and not somewhere else, that you are when you are and not somewhen else? Standing expresses the miracle of particularity, which in a universe emerging from an infinite ground of being manifesting in infinite ways with an infinite oneness is truly a miracle. How amazing that in the presence of God, we are also. I stand as me and only me here and now because of God's grace and will; I emerge from a sacred, creative act. Is this not a powerful place to be? Am I not in my simple standing in the presence of the holy? Am I not a miracle?

When I stand, I am the sacred circle, the magical circle, the circle of all relations. When I stand I am the exclamation point of a holy intent.

Standing, I am a landmark of the divine by which others may find their way, just as they are landmarks for me. Standing, I am a place of revelation. Standing, I am a point from which a line may emerge, from which a web may be made, from which a solid may be formed. I am the beginning of all geometry.

Standing is the primal creative act. God stands, and from God all emerges. I stand, and from me worlds may emerge as well. God and I stand together. When I stand, God and I are together.

Standing has nothing to do with liking or disliking where I am or when I am. Standing is not the opposite of sitting or lying down. I can sit or lie down and still be inwardly standing. Standing is not a posture; it is an affirmation of being that can unlock my power to co-create and to transform where and when I am.

All spiritual work begins from a source. Usually in spiritual terms, we identify this source as God or the Void or some such label for the generative mystery of creation. But for the work I do, I am the source. In a world of the particular and the specific, I am particular and specific. I do not mean by this that I take God's place, only that as a miracle, as a holy place defined by my standing, I am that mystery individuated; I am the source anchored in time and place, my time and my place. And so are you. We are sources together.

So, to begin our world work, we begin with the simple act of standing, our feet on the floor or on the ground, our bodies upright. We are the wizard's staff. We are the rainbow bridge connecting heaven and earth. We are the lightning rod that anchors the power of the heavens. But standing is not a posture alone; it is an inner place of silence, stillness, poise, balance; a place of rising up and sinking down, a place of being; a holy place, a sacred place, a miracle. It is a place of affirmation of our incarnation with all its potentials.

Think of it this way: that all movement begins with being still, that all lines and geometries begin with a point, that all possibilities begin with a source, that all rituals and magic begin with intent. In standing, you are that stillness, that point, that source, that intent.

Notes & Reflections

Exercise Three:
Standing

This exercise is very simple.

Take some time just to stand.

Stand up. Sit down. Then stand up again.

Take note of the phenomenon of standing itself. Don't try initially to move energy up and down your spine or your extremities; that is another exercise altogether. Energy is already moving up and down, through and around you just as you are standing. What you want to do is to pay attention to them. Pay attention to your self and where you are. Feel the reality, the solidity, the practicality, the specificity of your standing.

Think of some of the things I've said about your self and what it means to stand. Think of things I might have said. Say your own things. Appreciate yourself. Be present. Sink into your physicality. Feel how just standing can be relaxing. Feel yourself catching up with yourself.

After awhile—how long is up to you—standing may become wearying. Feel free to sit down or even lie down. Your body doesn't care what position it's in in order to be here and now. It is "standing" even when it is not upright. Be gentle with yourself.

In fact, stand some, sit some, and lie some and feel the difference. Chances are you will feel a power in standing, a declaration of beingness, that may not be as powerful in other positions. Or you may feel something quite different. I have certainly felt power when I sit cross-legged on the ground, gathering the energies, gathering my presence, gathering my world into my lap, as it were. So who am I to predict what you may feel? Experiment.

Remember that you don't have to do anything. Standing is a position of poise from which you can move in any direction, step anywhere, do anything. A field of possible movements and directions surrounds you: forward, back, right, left, up, down. In this potential of movement and action lies power. Feel into that power. Experiment with moving a step in this direction, a step in that. Everything you do with power begins with this simple movement from center; everything begins with a step, whether that step is one of body, mind, heart, or soul. From the point, infinite lines may radiate, geometries may emerge, and worlds may be shaped. All of this is in you as you stand. Feel into it. Think into it. Intuit into it.

You can be in any outer situation—moving, running, sitting, lying, talking, feeling, building, watching—and still be "standing." Use the power of your physicality to instruct your mind and heart in the power and sensation of standing, and let your standing be the wizard's staff along which your soul flows into your life.

Take time to stand. Stand and locate yourself. Stand and be holy. Stand and be potential waiting to be unleashed.

That is the exercise. Keep notes of anything you experience as you do this, any sensations, images, intuitions, insights, and so forth.

Exercise Three (Variation): Standing

This exercise has physical, mental, emotional, and spiritual aspects to it. These aspects are designed to be done all at once, but I'll present them as separate categories.

Physical:

The physical action of this exercise is simple. From a sitting position, you simply stand up. Be aware of the physical sensation and felt sense of standing. Feel the work of your body, the power of balance that keeps you upright. If you are already standing, become aware that you are standing and be mindful of the felt sense of standing. If you are physically unable to stand, you can still assume an inner attitude of standing, perhaps simply by straightening your spine as much as possible.

Emotional:

Feel the power of being upright. Feel the strength of rising up against the gravity of the earth. Feel how standing singles you out and expresses your individuality. You stand for what you believe you stand up to be counted. Standing proclaims that you are here. Feel the strength and presence of your identity and sovereignty.

Mental:

Celebrate your humanness. You are an upright being. You emerge from the mass of nature, from the vegetative and animal states into a realm of thinking and imagining. In standing, you hands are released from providing locomotion. Feel the freedom of your hands that don't have to support you but can now be used to create, manipulate, touch, and express your thoughts and imagination.

Magical:

When you stand, your spine becomes a magical staff, the *axis mundi* (center) of your personal world, generating the field that embraces you. The spine is the traditional wizard's staff along which dragon power flows and the centers of energy sing in resonance with the cosmos.

Spiritual:

Standing, you are the incarnate link between heaven and earth. Your energy rises into the sky and descends into the earth. Light descends and ascends, swirling along your spine in a marriage of matter and spirit. This energy is both personal and the transpersonal, giving birth to something new, something human, individual and unique. In doing this exercise of Standing, you stand. As you do so, work through these levels of sensation, feeling, thought, energy, and spirit, appreciating the power, the freedom, the sovereignty, and the presence emerging from the simple act of standing. When you have finished doing it, record your experiences in your journal. Do this recording each time you do this exercise, so you can see what emerges for you over a period of time.

Notes & Reflections

Chapter Four:
Buffering

Here we explore the concept and practice of "buffering."

A couple I once knew back in the sixties had purchased a water bed. One night he got a painful cramp in his leg which caused him to leap out of bed. As he did so, he created a wave which swept across the bed, lifted up his wife, and dumped her out of bed on the other side! The next day they upgraded their bed to one that had baffles in it, small strips of wood and plastic that broke up any waves that might form.

An important part of world work is being such a baffle ourselves (not just baffled!) and helping to break up psychic waves of anger, hatred, fear, and the like which can sweep across our world. I think of this as being a buffer, and it is also important when we seek to connect with some challenging area in our lives or in the larger world. We want whatever negative energies we encounter to be broken up and transmuted and not passed on by us. We want to break up any resonance that might be there, either in us or in the environment, to so negative states.

Doing this is the next step after standing. When we stand, we affirm our power, but we also affirm our state of being. We are putting ourselves up to stand in the currents of energy in the world and buffer them or act as baffles that prevent negative energies from being passed on. To do this, we must not be reactive ourselves.

This state might be seen as one of neutrality or impersonality, but both of these are usually experienced as emotions. The buffering state is neither emotional nor mental. It is a proactive, radiant spiritual state rooted in love. Think of a Teflon barrier. Negative energies can't stick to it and can't pass it either. The charge of their momentum is lost and they can be dealt with more easily.

This is certainly a state of calm in which our own energy is kept free from agitation and the possibility of resonance. It is not a passive state, like just being a baffle in a water bed, but an active one. It is something we do, not just something we are. It is holding and heightening a certain kind of energy which in its own way transmutes energies of negativity that might impact upon us.

This is what we want to explore next.

In doing world work, four things are very important:

• Our alignment with spiritual resources that can help and make a difference, whether those resources are within our personal selves or within transpersonal sources. Basically, if we're going to go fire-fighting, do we have a source of water with us?

• A clear vision of what we are doing, liberally mixed with the humility that comes from realizing that we don't have all the information about the situation and that things are not always what they seem.

• A clear presentation of the presence/energies that we wish to contribute to a situation for its most wholesome resolution; do those energies or does that presence clearly and wholly live in us during the time of our world working?

• A capacity to not take on or react to whatever negative or powerful emotional and mental energies may be present in the situation; in effect, we do not want to be shaped and seduced by the situation itself, becoming part of it rather than a force to enable it to transform itself.

Buffering is an expression of this last capacity, though it is rooted in the other three as well.

We can "take on" and ultimately end up contributing to the less-than-wholesome or helpful energies of a situation in a variety of ways. Here are two main ways:

One:

We become caught up in the vibrations of the thoughts and feelings emanating from the situation. The outer layers of our own energy fields or auras are constantly responding to psychic energies in our environment and are always in motion unless we take steps to calm ourselves and ensure that our energy field takes its cue from our inner being.

Think of ourselves as small lakes connected by canals to each other. When a wave comes through the canal from someone else, it can set our water moving, carrying that wave forward and into all the other canals to which we are connected. To prevent this, the wave must be counteracted in some manner; it must be buffered and "baffled," just like the wave in my friends' water bed.

Of course, this picture is simplistic. Still we can and do often pass on wave-forms of thought and emotion. Here is a common example. Someone in our family gets into a snit (an esoteric term for Sustaining Negative Impulses and Thoughts!). The energy around that person gets moody, irritable, angry, depressed, whatever. Before long, others in the family are acting moodily, with irritation or anger, or are feeling depressed, all for no particular outer reason. Soon, the whole family is beginning to react until one of us realizes that we've all taken on one person's energy in a kind of sympathetic resonance and acts to change his or her personal energy: to opt out of the cloud of despondence, so to speak, and to change the energy mood and atmosphere.

At work we may be with a colleague who is out of sorts and unless we are careful, we can find ourselves getting out of sorts, too.

Terrorists strike New York and suddenly everyone in the country is afraid and seeing terrorists lurking behind every bush and corner in their neighborhoods.

The thing about taking on energy from outside oneself in this manner is that the emotions and thoughts we may then feel and have often have no direct relationship to anything happening in our immediate environment. We are caught up in an imaginal world and begin projecting its characteristics upon the immediate reality around us.

The simple fact is that we can be energetically shaped and molded by our environment, at least in surface ways. Unless we are mindful, those surface feelings and thoughts, though, can be taken as our own and acted upon, which can have the effect of "passing the wave."

Two:

We can be "shaped" by the energies of the situation. This shaping is different from simply echoing those energies and passing them on.

We are shaped when a part of ourselves is automatically evoked by the situation. This part is usually a self-image, a personal "imaginel," that seems appropriate to the situation. (I use the term "imaginel," to mean a thought/emotion-form with a certain directional force and charge of its own. This is not just a metaphor. Thoughts and emotions in the subtle worlds are things, objective and possessing of form.)

For example, when someone describes to me a problem they are having, I have a tendency to become a Fixer, to take on a pattern of emotions and thoughts that cluster around the image of being a person who can fix everything and make things right. But the Fixer is not a part of me that actually CAN fix anything; it is a part of me that exists because of the situation, if that makes sense to you. There is problem, and there is fixer. But when I become the Fixer, I am being shaped and defined by the energies of the problem.

Now this is subtle, because I may indeed wish to fix and be able to fix the problem, but I don't want to do so as a Fixer. The Fixer is an automatic response and may not contain within itself the knowledge or skill that is really needed by the situation. The Fixer becomes defined by the situation and may lack the capacity or flexibility to think "outside the box" about the situation to come up with innovative ideas or insights. Thus, if the situation is about money, the Fixer thinks of problem-solving in terms of money.

These personal imaginels or thought-forms can seem positive or negative. They can be wonderful self-images like the Rescuing Knight, the Fixer, the Compassionate One, the Healer, etc., or they can be negative like the Disempowered One, the Failure, the "This Is Beyond Me" persona, the Hider, the Retreater, and so forth. These imaginels are habits of thought and feeling which get triggered by the energy of situations, because in effect they are themselves complexes of energy lodged within our personality field. (Some clairvoyants claim to see these thought-forms in people's auras, but I've never had that experience, so I can't speak to it.)

I know these thought-forms can be considered in psychological terms, but here I am thinking of them as energy complexes. This is important.

Let's look at the anatomy of an emotion. An emotion has an energy component, which is tied into the neurophysiology of the body and into

41

specific chemical constituencies. It also can have a mental component which consists of whatever images, vague or otherwise, memories or otherwise, are evoked by that energy. And it can have what I think of as a Root, which is its connection to a deeper part of ourselves, the empersonal spirit or incarnate spiritual part of us, and even deeper into the soul itself.

Most of our emotions during a day do not have Roots but they do have energy and hence can energize us and motivate us in various ways. Many emotions have mental content or associated images. Fewer emotions have Roots.

Having Roots really means that the energy of the emotion (NOT its mental content) can extend beyond the physical/emotional field of frequency and vibration and extend into the field of the soul. This does not necessarily make the emotion stronger or more impactful, but it does give it depth and a sense of rising beyond the immediate situation. For example, joy and happiness are two different things, seen esoterically and mystically. Happiness is an emotion that may have little or no roots. One is happy in a given situation, but if the situation changes, the happiness can be lost. The energy of emotions is more often than not situation dependent or tied to some set of physical circumstances or structures (these can be physiological structures). But joy remains even under circumstances of great distress, pain, turmoil, loss, and so forth. It is Being-Dependent, not Situation-Dependent.

In some spiritual teachings, joy is considered a quality, not an emotion. This is certainly my experience. I have the same ups and downs of happiness/sadness as everyone else, but I also have a continuous sense of joy that transcends any situation I may be in.

We will come back to this distinction later, as it is important in world work.

I'm sure all of this sounds very commonplace and familiar. It is certainly part of the experience of all of us. We all know how some feelings last and others are transient.

In the context of buffering, though, we need to go beyond this sense of familiarity and look (and feel) more deeply. It can be obvious when we suddenly pick up a feeling tone or a mood or an emotion that we know is not ours. If I attune to the sniper currently terrorizing the area around our nation's capital, I will feel fear. I can tune into the fear that he or she is generating. I have enough awareness to know that this fear is not a part of my life here in the other Washington, thousands of miles away. I do not fear that I will step out of my house and be shot by a sniper. I can feel the energy of the fear the sniper is generating and also realize it is not MY fear.

But the complexes of thought/energy/emotions that are our personal habitual thought forms are something else. We identify with them more completely. They seem like ourselves. But if we pay attention, we can see how we put them on and off at different times depending on the situation around us. This is more than just taking on a role, by the way. It is a genuine manifestation of a presence of energy within our overall incarnate field. While we are in it, it IS us and we ARE it. It is more than a role.

The problem with these imaginels is that they do not have Roots. They seem like us, but they are really not us. Because of this, they do not have access to the deeper, more rooted energies, feelings, thoughts, etc. that do arise from our levels of wholeness and spirit. Like any habit, they can be useful at times but at other times, they only get in our way.

In the context of World Work, when we deliberately attune to a world situation and to its energy and we find that energy distressing, even if we have enough awareness and presence of mind not to take on that energy and pass it on, we may not realize that we can be drawn into the larger energy system of that situation through a personal thought form that is evoked by it. We cease to be ourselves in our wholeness and rootedness in spirit and become an "Identity Imaginel." In so doing, we become in subtle (and sometimes no so subtle ways) a part of the problem. We participate in and perpetuate the very energies we want to diminish and transmute.

This is why I counsel people who are going to do World Work not to approach it with the attitude of being a "spiritual warrior" or "a Light Worker" or any other such attitude or image. Such images ultimately restrict us, even though they may be inspiring images of power and calling. They don't let us be ourselves in the fullest way and can actually cut us off from our deep roots. Such images can carry their own reserves or resources of energy but these can turn out to be insufficient for really dealing with the problem.

A metaphor would be a fireman who carries all his water in a tank on his back rather than having a hose to plug into the water main. That water in the tank will be useful up to a point, but fighting a large fire, it will quickly become exhausted. And worse, the fireman may be persuaded that he has more resources to draw upon and is thus more capable than he really is. The tank on his back gives a sense of power, but it is limited power.

I'd like you to think about this. This is a subtle thing, but important. It is one of the ways we can fail to buffer. We don't spread the negative energy, but we can be drawn into participating and helping to co-create the situation that is producing the negative energy. We don't spread it but we don't dissipate it either.

Notes & Reflections

_____

_____

_____

_____

_____

_____

_____

_____

_____

_____

_____

_____

_____

_____

Exercise Four:
Buffering

Let's begin with a simple exercise.

For the next two days or so, I want you to observe your reactions to negative news stories. I would like you to deliberately seek out (or at least not actively avoid) troublesome news, whether on TV, on the radio, or in print. I want you to expose yourself to material that has a good likelihood of making you feel agitated, angry, possibly fearful, and the like. As you do encounter and engage with this material, observe your own reactions. Whatever emotions arise, where are you feeling them? How is your body reacting? What thoughts arise? How do thoughts and feelings feed each other to magnify their effect? Please note your responses.

Notes & Reflections

_____

_____

_____

_____

_____

_____

_____

_____

_____

_____

_____

Chapter three: Buffering continued ....

Now we will explore the how-tos of energetic buffering.

OK, how do we buffer. There is more than one way, and ultimately, there are probably as many ways as there are individuals. The basic act of buffering is to say, "I stand in my own energy, not in anyone or anything else's, and I determine the nature and quality of the energy that enters my world." It is an expression of sovereignty.

In a broad way, then, whatever helps me to understand and affirm and then to express my unique personhood and to choose to bring positive, fostering, and blessing-ful energies into my world serves the act of buffering. Be on the look out for those things that help you to do this.

Over the years I have used four techniques, which have evolved in a somewhat progressive way. These are not unique or new techniques by any means. They are practiced quite widely and will be very familiar to you. These four are Alignment, Substitution, Neutrality, and Radiance. They can be used in combination with each other quite easily.

Before I discuss these four, however, I have a preliminary thought about the nature of emotional and mental energies that we have already discussed. I find it very helpful to distinguish between the energy or feel of an emotion or thought and its content. This distinction can be subtle, since feel and content can certainly affect each other, but with practice, you can tell the difference.

A good way is to look at what the emotion or thought feels like in your body and in your vital energy. Does it make me feel more vital or does it make me feel tired? Is it locatable in a particular place in my body?

I feel fear, for example, in the pit of my stomach, in the solar plexus. By putting my attention on the physical sensation, it alters how I experience my fear. The content of the physical sensation replaces the mental content, all the images of the things I am afraid of. I focus on sensation rather than on image.

When I am buffering, what I am buffering is not really an emotion or a thought, though it can generate such within me and it may be transmitted to me in an emotional or mental way. What I am buffering is energy, the motive element, the part of the thought or emotion that makes it dynamic and causes it to move from one person to another, from one place in my bodymind to another, from one region in the world to another, and so forth. I may wish to deal with the content as well, but my first task is to get it to stand still, so to speak: to render it inert.

In the exercises, we end up looking at that energy as a kind of "eel" moving in the fluid nature of our subtle fields. By calming everything down, by exerting control over my subtle energy field, I can render this energy, this "eel" inert. I can experience it as something separate from me. It is an "imaginel," a thought/emotion-form, as we have discussed.

Again, this is not just a metaphor. Thoughts and emotions in the subtle worlds are things, every bit as objective and possessing of form as chairs and tables and lampposts and ferrets are for us in our everyday world. It is a familiar phrase in occultism and esoteric or metaphysical thought to say that "thoughts are things," but we don't always fully grasp the implications of this. Thoughts and emotions are experienced by our everyday mind as being subjective but are seen by inner sight as being objective.

The art of buffering depends greatly on the ability to realize this and to see the objective side of thoughts and emotions.

While you are working on the exercises, let me go over the four techniques of alignment, substitution, neutrality, and Radiance. These are by no means exclusive and can be used in any combination, more or less. But they are distinctive.

Alignment is the process through which I link my energy field and consciousness with that of another source so that my personal field is augmented by that relationship.

The simplest and most common form of this technique in Christian circles, for example, is "I do this in the Name of Christ," accompanied by an earnest attempt to attune to the presence and energy of the Christ. In the case of buffering, the prayer might be more like "I stand in the Light of the Christ," or "I am filled with the Christ light" or something like that.

Alignment is attuning to a source of spiritual help and power that in your estimation and experience contains the kind of energy you would wish to have with which to deal with the situation confronting you. It is calling upon a spiritual ally.

In the case of buffering, you are calling upon an inner ally or spiritual source to help you withstand or transform a negative energy which is impacting upon you. It comes to help you stand in the midst of that energy and not take it on or succumb to it, whether that energy is fear, anger, hostility, or whatever. You are aligning with the helpful and transformative quality or qualities with which you associate this ally or source.

Alignment can have another meaning, too. It can mean aligning with spiritual qualities within yourself as well. The qualities you wish to invoke in order to stand and buffer negative energies don't need to come from an outside source. They can come from within you, from your soul or empersonal spirit, for instance, or from your sense of your sacredness.

Whether your attention turns inward or outward or both, alignment is the technique of putting yourself in sync with a vibration and energy different from the one you are trying to buffer, one that will be helpful to you and to the situation.

Substitution is the process, as the name suggests, of putting one thing in the place of another. In this case, you are identifying the particular energy that you are buffering and you replace it with its opposite or with an energy or quality that is similar to it but a bit further along towards a more positive quality.

For example, you are encountering an energy of anger. If you can, you can hold that energy and replace it with a quality of peace or forgiveness or calmness.

However, it may be difficult to leap directly from anger to peace. The angry energy itself may (and probably will) resist turning into its opposite. So instead of peace, you replace it with amused irritation or loving concern or some other quality which is less hurtful and negative than the anger but which is not quite full peacefulness and calm either. Humor is an excellent quality to bring into this substitution process, because it takes the sting out and puts the energy into a larger perspective or context.

Neutrality is just that, holding a neutral quality that is not ruffled or disturbed by the energy you are experiencing. You are detached and observant. The incoming energy cannot find any vibration in you to which it can attach or which it can use to propagate itself. It's as if in our metaphor of connected lakes, you become land instead of water, so the wave of energy has no medium through which to travel. It meets your neutrality and stops.

True neutrality is not exactly detachment or a "I-don't care, I'm-not-involved" attitude. It is holding your center, your identity, your energy in a non-reflective state that simply doesn't resonate to the energy coming in from the environment. Neutrality is not non-engagement, or even non-participation, but a clarity of one's own sovereignty, energy, and identity so that you cannot be "co-opted" to reflect, reproduce, or resonate with any quality or energy which you do not mindfully choose to be your expression.

The energy exercises largely focus on this quality of neutrality.

Radiance is the most active form of buffering. You are not simply stopping an energy or blocking it; you are not even just changing it, as in substitution. You are in effect consuming it. The image is of you as a sun whose light and heat consume whatever falls into its aura.

In this context, you are actively and mindfully radiating a chosen quality of your own, backed up by your own will and love. If you pick up a negative emanation from the environment, it does not change what you radiate. It is absorbed by it, so to speak, and dissipated in the strength of whatever quality you are putting forth.

Radiance can be seen as a technique, something to do when you feel the presence of negative energies impacting upon you. But its true power comes from it not being a one-off kind of event. We radiate from our integrity and from the way we naturally comport ourselves through our day. It is the outflow of our beingness. Radiance is something we can cultivate whether we are in contact with anything negative, hurtful, suffering, or not. It gains in strength and naturalness the more we do cultivate it and see ourselves as stars of human luminosity and love.

Exercise Five:
Part A, Feeling Energy

This exercise is not exactly about buffering but about feeling energy (whether emotional, mental, vital, physical or combinations thereof) differently.

Imagine yourself inside an egg made of water. This water has varying layers of density, which you could picture as being of different colors. You can picture as many layers between you and the surface as you wish, but there should be at least four: the surface layer, the subsurface layer, a deeper layer, and the deepest layer which immediately surrounds you.

The surface layer is the least dense and is capable of rapid movement and change. As you move inward, each succeeding layer becomes more dense and less easily moved until the layer closest to you is very still and calm and not easily ruffled.

The "you" in this exercise is a point of experience, a point of view, rather than an historical and autobiographical self. It is just you as a point where experience and awareness happen. We need not get very metaphysical and philosophical about this!

When winds come from the surrounding world, the outer layer of your watery egg responds easily. Waves and ripples can form and move about the surface of your egg. Each of these waves and ripples carries energy which can mimic or is the result of energies that have touched you from the environment, just as the surface of a pond forms waves when touched by a wind blowing across it.

Depending on the power of these waves, they can induce similar patterns in the subsurface level, and in deeper levels. If they are very powerful, they can even disturb the calm water immediately surrounding you. But whether the energy disturbs and is registered in the entire egg or only upon its surface, the point of this exercise is to realize that it is the water that is agitated, not you.

The first part of this exercise is to picture this egg very clearly. Please note that this is NOT an accurate picture of the aura that surrounds each of us, only a metaphorical image. The point of the image is to say that we are immersed in a field that responds to environmental conditions. Reactions in this field can be taken personally, but in this exercise we want to see that they need not be. They are only reactions and vibrations in a field of energy, an "egg of water," and not part of us.

So visualize yourself within this field, this egg, as clearly as you can.

Now, once you have done that and are comfortable with this perception, I would like you to think of something that causes you to react emotionally (and mentally, too). It need not be something to which you react strongly, that is, to start with, you may not want to pick a strong emotion to deal with...and it need not be a negative emotion, though in the practice of buffering that is usually what we are working with.

As you feel this emotion, see it as a ripple somewhere in your egg. If it's just a minor thing, you may see it rippling away on the surface layer; if it affects you more deeply, see it rippling away in one of the deeper layers. The key element here is that you see this emotion or thought as existing in your subtle energy field, not in you. You generate this field but you are not this field.

In this exercise, you are seeking to experience two things: an emotion (or a thought, it works for those, too) as an energy active in your subtle field, causing ripples and waves, and yourself as distinct from that field. You are not the watery egg or the energetic field that surrounds you. You are something else. Just what that is doesn't matter to this exercise: call yourself a witnessing point of view, if you wish. In this sense, this is an exercise in detachment.

Once you are comfortable with the experience of having emotions and thoughts as energy forms in your subtle field or aura but not being those emotions and thoughts, then we can move to the next stage of this exercise.

In this stage, you become an active center of calmness and or energy. Instead of the watery egg responding only to what blows across it or into it from the environment, now you are going to experience how it responds to you.

Again, see yourself at the center of this watery egg, and, thinking of some situation or person that generates an emotional response for you, see that response as an energy wave moving through the water of the egg at some layer or other.

Once you have a sense that you are in the center and the emotion (or thought) is a ripple in the field, use your will and imagination to calm the waters throughout the egg. See all ripples being smoothed out and calmed moving from the innermost layer of water out to the surface. Hold your watery egg in your calming presence, just as if you are holding it in your hands and preventing it from shaking and vibrating. (Energetically speaking, you are visualizing holding your emotional, mental, and vital energy fields in the larger field of your soul.) Just see calmness moving throughout the egg, throughout all the subtle fields of your incarnate self and personality. See and feel the water losing its agitation and calming down.

Once you have everything calmed down, observe what this feels like. What has happened to the emotional charge that you were feeling earlier?

Exercise Five:
Part B, Calming a wriggling eel

Now we're going to do this a little differently. Now we're going to imagine that the emotion or thought you were experiencing rippling through the water of your egg is not just a wind-induced phenomenon, not only a ripple, but something like a wriggly fish or eel. Instead of wind rippling your egg, someone or something is dropping eels into your water, and it is their wiggling about that is causing the ripples.

When you calm the water, you calm the eel so that it effectively falls asleep or is otherwise immobilized. This allows you to examine this creature without it moving about and churning things up. You can examine its structure: what kind of emotion-eel or thought-eel is it? What is its content? What is motivating it? What kind of ecology does it come from?

In this variant of the exercise, you are not just banishing the emotion or thought by calming it out of existence, but you are observing it without it being able to agitate you or your surroundings.

Notes & Reflections

Practice this—indeed, practice all the stages of this exercise so far—and note what comes up for you.

Now I want to present the next stage of this exercise. It will be easy since some of you are probably already doing it.

But first, a word from our sponsor...uh..no... I mean, first a comment on what we've done so far.

In spiritual and psychological studies, we are familiar with the witnessing state in which a person detaches from subjective content and simply observes it. The exercise we are doing here is similar to that, but it is not identical. It can have a similar effect of inducing calm, but there are two major differences between the witnessing state and what we are working with here.

The first is that in this exercise we are working with the energy of an emotion or thought and not just its content. It isn't so much that I witness content going by but that I feel into the energy at work in my field. Here, the task is more one of active sensing than it is of just observing. Think of a scientist with a meter to detect the nature and strength of an electromagnetic field or a Geiger counter to detect the presence and strength of radiation.

You are dealing with a thought or an emotion not as an artifact of consciousness but as something akin to an electromagnetic or radioactive phenomenon. It is more of a psychic exercise than a witnessing one and draws on a different set of skills (and everyone has the psychic skills to do this).

Of course, the content of a thought or emotion is not totally separable form the quality and intensity of its energy. These are tied together and influence each other. But especially in dealing with negative or repulsive images and energies, if I can psychically go past the image and my reaction to it to evaluate and deal with its energy directly, then I have a tool both for protecting myself and for affecting that energy in positive ways.

Second, in this exercise we are seeing thoughts and emotions not simply as subjective content, something happening our heads, but as real objects within the "frequency worlds" usually referred to as the astral and mental planes. This gives an objectivity to our witnessing, just as if we were observing the furniture and other contents of our living rooms. These thoughts and emotions have shape and substance and effect.

Once I went into a store to visit a friend of mine who worked there. I immediately felt tension in the air. When my friend walked out from a back room, psychically she looked like a porcupine with its quills all erect. There were actual spikes of energy of varying lengths protruding from her auric field, which itself was suffused with a blood red color. It is rare for me to have such a distinct clairvoyant perception, but I could feel those spikes impinging on me! It was psychically and even physically painful, and I had to steel myself to approach her.

My friend was prone to irritability anyway due to stresses in her life at that time, but she was obviously having a worse than usual morning and had become Porcupine Woman. I immediately whisked her out of the store (she was due for a coffee break; she was also the manager) and took her down to a nearby coffee shop where we simply talked and I could get her laughing. By the time she went back to work, the quills and spikes had vanished.

Anyone could have noticed my friend was angry and irritable, and many people would have felt the impact of her energy somewhere in their bodies (usually the solar plexus which is where so many of us register emotional energy). What they might not have realized is that her energy WAS impacting their subtle bodies just as if she had punched them physically or had jabbed spikes into them. There was real, objective component to this experience, not only a subjective one.

A person need not be psychic or clairvoyant to make use of this knowledge. Just realizing that "thoughts are things," as the old saying goes, can begin to shift one's attention and attitude, perception and perspective. In our case, it help us in world work to realize that we are working in a realm of real objects—thought forms, emotion forms, combining into what I have termed imaginels (but feel free to use your own terminology)—and that these real objects can be manipulated and dealt with just as you would move furniture around a room or put out a fire or light a candle.

So, in this next stage of this exercise, we are going to go from observing and calming to actively radiating and altering: a work of transformation.

Exercise Five:
Part C, The magical candle

Step One:

As before, we are going to do this exercise in two steps. In both steps, I would like you to continue to use the overall image of the watery egg, though if you wish to be more precise, consider the egg as a fluid field or just as a field. As in all such exercises, though, the important thing is that the image or images you work with should feel natural and comfortable to you. Once you get the gist of what I want you to do, please feel ok about changing the images if you wish and substituting any comparable images with which you may feel more comfortable.

In the first step, once again see an energy entering your field; you can see it as a wave or as an eel or fish, (or as something else, if you wish), but as before your objective is to calm your field so that the emotion or thought or both is caught, so to speak.

Now this time, imagine that at the center of your egg where you are is a magical aromatherapy candle. When you light it, you will be radiating into your egg not just light and warmth but the quality of the aroma as well. In this case, we will make this quality one of love. The effect of lighting it will be that throughout your egg, the water is no longer just a neutral fluid but now a positive, radiant presence of that quality, which in this case is love. Your field is not just receptive, it is "pro-ceptive" as well. It doesn't just register, it also acts to transform what it registers into its own dominant quality.

In effect, you are radiating love throughout your auric field, suffusing your energy field with it, like sunlight shafting through the clear waters of a lagoon, giving everything the glow of a new light.

What does this feel like? What effect does this have on the wave or eel that has entered your field? You are now not just calming and capturing it, but you are subjecting it to another energy of your choosing. What happens?

Please give this a try before we go on to the second step.

Step Two:

I want to continue now to the second step of this exercise. You have been practicing with radiance, of filling your field with the "aroma" of your "inner candle." Now we are going to be a bit more aggressive and proactive.

In this step we are not simply suffusing our auras with a particular quality. Now you are going to create an alternative quality or imaginel to substitute for and replace the disturbing one you have been working with.

This may seem like a purely imaginative exercise, but it is a very real process upon that realm in which thoughts and emotions are things and not just "feelings" or "ideas."

As before, bring to your mind some situation that can bombard you with potentially negative or upsetting energies and images. Heaven knows, the news is filled with them!

Once you have identified that energy (that "imagin-eel" that will enter your field), consider what other quality, image, or energy would transform it into its opposite, i.e. love for hate or peace for anger or courage for fear, or compassion for suffering.

You are going to build a thought-form made up of that opposite energy and superimpose it onto the disturbed energy. This is not quite the same as the substitution model I mentioned for buffering, for here you are not simply buffering but actively transforming and reforming an energy.

Think of it this way. Instead of an eel, think of the negative or disturbed energy as a metal ore which has a particular shape. Through your radiance as practiced in the previous step, you are going to melt that ore until it loses its shape and simply flows. In practical terms, this means you are holding onto the energy itself (the flowing, molten part) but consuming its "shape," (the mental content of that energy). Then you are going to pour that melted ore into a new mold, just as if you had melted down gold ingots and were not pouring the molten gold into a mold for a necklace or a statue.

You are transferring the energy itself from one form which has been shaped by the environment into another form that you create.

Notes & Reflections

Before I give you an example, let's talk about creating the new form, the mold into which the energy will be poured.

You have two sources to draw upon here, and you can use both. One is the transpersonal dimension, particularly as represented by your sense of the sacred. The other is the "empersonal" dimension, represented by your sense of yourself as a compassionate, spiritual person.

[EMPERSONAL SPIRIT: This is a word I coined to mean "that spirit (or spiritual energy) that emerges from the personal and through the personal." I contrast it with spiritual energy descending from the transpersonal. The empersonal spirit is created as we first engage with the Incarnate Realm, much like a spark is struck when flint strikes steel. It is an emergence from the interaction of the spiritual energies of the Incarnate Soul with the energies of the Incarnate Realm. This empersonal spirit grows with us through our lifetime, fed by our learning, our efforts to gain wisdom, our accomplishments, all the positive actions that we undertake, our attunements, and so forth. It is a spiritual source within us in addition to and complementary to the spiritual energies that can come from transpersonal levels of our being. It manifests through our personal identity and is a gift of spirit, an energy of spirit, unique to this realm, like local currency.]

Empersonal and transpersonal energies blend and interact, but they are not identical, at least as far as I understand them.

Let us say I want to build a "mold" of love. I bring to mind my sense of what the love of the sacred is like. What attributes, what qualities, what manifestation does this love have? I can use images, stories, words, and so forth from one or more spiritual traditions to help me visualize this. For instance, how do I imagine Jesus Christ loving or Buddha? How does the Goddess love?

I want and need to incorporate this transpersonal sense into my mold because it represents a broader, deeper, more universal aspect of the quality I am creating than what I may offer from my own personal experience alone.

But I also want to incorporate what love means to me as a person. What is my unique, individual experience and understanding of love?

How have I loved in the past? How do I love? What is love like to me not just as a universal quality but as a specific one alive and potent in my life?

I want to have this personal element in my mold since I am a person and it is through my personal, unique engagement with life that the universal attains specific focus and power in the moment.

So I am building in my mind and heart an "image" of what love is, both transpersonally and personally. That image will have a shape within me. This is not necessarily a visual shape but a feeling shape, a felt sense.

If you want to do a little side exercise to explore this, hold your hands in a cupped fashion as if you were holding water in them, or hold them side by side about seven inches or so apart. Imagine you are holding love in your palms or between your hands, as if it were a ball or some other object. Imagine what love is like to you transpersonally. What does it feel like in your palms or between your hands? What shape does it have?

Imagine what love is like personally to you. What does it feel like in your palms or between your hands? What shape does it have?

Put the two together: empersonal/transpersonal love. What does it feel like in your palms or between your hands? What shape does it have?

Try this a few times and see what happens.

In creating this "mold," I can certainly call on allies or I can imaginatively and contemplatively put myself into the presence of a sacred presence. For instance, I can imagine myself being with Jesus or Buddha and exploring what that feels like. What does it feel like to be loved by one of these beings? Who would I be under Jesus' loving gaze, embraced by his presence? What would be revealed to me about love?

However, I do it, I want to build this mold of love (or peace or courage or whatever the quality/energy may be) in a way that blends both transpersonal and personal elements.

Once I have this mold or image, I superimpose it over the energy that I have held in my radiance. I will the energy to fill this mold; I invite it to do so. I take the motive power of that imaginel which I have been working—not its mental content but its motive, energetic power—and pour it imaginatively into my own image. If hatred has this much energy, then now love has that same amount of energy. Then I release it in its new form to return to its source or I can commit it to angelic or supersensory allies, or simply to the sacred, to use in whatever way serves the highest good of all.

Here's a simple example of something like this transformation of energy from one shape to another. People who do public speaking or performances are quite familiar with the energy of anxiety and even fear that we call "stage fright." I know that even after nearly forty years now of public work, I still feel it before every lecture, every workshop, every event.

Examination of this fright reveals that it has two aspects. One is the pure energy of it, experienced usually as sensation in the body. The other is its mental content, which is usually a set of images of all the things that can go wrong, of being humiliated, of being rejected by audiences, and so forth. What I, and many other public speakers, have learned is to ignore and throw away the latter, the mental content—the original shape and mold of the fright—but to hold onto the energy. The energy enlivens us, it gives us juice which we can pour into our speaking or performance. It is the images which are frightening and which evoke fearful responses from within me; the energy is just energy, and as such, I can feed on it and use it. I can cast it into another mold. When I step on stage in front of an audience, I feel perfectly calm, but I can feel the energy that a moment ago had been fear but which is now creativity coursing through me.

Here is an example.

You are watching the news, let us say, and you see something that disturbs you. You feel the possibility of this news event to broadcast fear into the collective. Perhaps it is bad economic news. Perhaps it is war news or a story of a violent crime.

Let us say that the energy you feel impinging upon you is fear. Immediately, you gather that energy into your field and irradiate it, surrounding it with your calm energy. You immobilize the "imagineel."

63

You will see upon examination that it is both an energy and it is mental content. The latter are all the images that are associated with the story, AND that arise from within us as inspired by the story ("this could happen to me or someone I love!" might be an example of such a thought).

Using your will and imagination, set the mental content aside. You need not think these thoughts or hold these images. Your mind is as vast as the cosmos, as filled with love as the sacred can pour itself into you.

Now, create your own subtle imaginel shape, shaped by your will and imagination from your own transpersonal and personal experiences. Let us make it a shape of peace and protection. Feel in your body what these qualities are like, what you feel like in experiencing them; let these qualities evoke new mental content, new images, memories, and the like. Shape a mold of peace and protection.

Now let the sensation of the energy that came from the fear and the news event flow into that mold, into your own imaginel. Breath out the energy you are holding into a mold of peace and protection. The news story has given you a gift! It has given you energy. Now this energy, plus whatever you wish to add to it, can be used to send peace and protection out into the collective.

Using this example, try it, and note what you experience.

Notes & Reflections

Chapter Five:
A Spiritual Tool Kit

In this chapter, we are going to explore elements in your spiritual tool kit—your "service kit"—before beginning the actual process of doing world work.

Buffering is a form of protection as well as of service. It is a service in that it allows you to be a presence that stops and even transforms negative, hurtful, depressed, angry, and fearful energies that you may find in your environment, impacting upon you from the collective consciousness of humanity, or arising from within yourself. It basically allows you to create a clear space around yourself which in turn can be projected out into your environment.

This clear space is also protective. It is not precisely "armor" but an active, transformative condition that manages and adjusts the energy forms that enter your field and move on from you out into the world.

The practice of buffering goes way beyond doing world work and is, I feel, an essential part of living our energistic lives; it is a form of spiritual hygiene. I felt that I could not really discuss world work, in which we deliberately place ourselves into negativity's way, without giving some instruction as to this more basic skill.

Buffering, while protective in nature in much the way that a good immune system is protective, is not a really a technique of protection per se, at least not to me. It is not the same as "raising shields" or "hardening the auric field," or banishing negative energies. If you are interested in techniques of psychic protection themselves, here are three books I would recommend: *Feeling Safe* and *Psychic Protection* by William Bloom, and *Psychic Shield: The Personal Handbook of Psychic Protection* by Caitlin Matthews.

We will touch a bit on protective techniques, but the kind of world work we are doing here should not require more than the usual kind of care and attention. As I said above, in world work we do put ourselves mindfully into negativity's way, but we are not trying to take on what might be termed conditions or forces of evil: very old, stuck, and powerful patterns of energy.

Dealing with the old, icky, slimy, dark stuff is the kind of work that we can be called to do as a soul's mission—and the calling comes from within and carries with it an instinctive sense of how to protect ourselves—but it is not something we just decide to do because we want to be "spiritual warriors." It requires a great deal of preparatory work, work on self, a discipline of inner attunement, and the like, just as a soldier goes through training. It is beyond what I can offer here in this class. It is also the kind of work that is never (or very rarely) done without spiritual allies. It is a partnership kind of work, not a solo one. The image of the spiritual and occult adept sallying forth to do battle with evil is fun for comic books but unrealistic and dangerous in real life, not to mention often ineffective as well.

So, while we will be exposing ourselves in world work to negative conditions of suffering, anger, hatred, fear and the like, these will not be beyond our ordinary capabilities to handle without resorting to unusual and extreme forms of inner protection. We will not be going up against "forces of evil" or negative energetic conditions that are deeply rooted, very powerful, and highly resistant to change. Should you in fact run up against something like that which makes you feel out of your depth and potentially overwhelmed, unless you have strong inner guidance to do otherwise, my best advice is to run! Stop whatever it is you are doing and break any connection that you have made with that condition or the environment in which it is manifesting. And call for help! Call to allies, to sacred beings, to the Sacred itself.

Doesn't that make you feel better and more secure? <grin>

Here is an analogy.

The kind of world work I refer to in this class is like going into a storm. There can be wind, rain, lightning, and you may feel buffeted, but you can handle it.

Going up against what I think of as planetary evil—the old, deeply rooted patterns of hurtful, destructive, and negative thought, feeling, and energy that have powerful and long-lasting momentum—is like going into a strong hurricane. You can do it, but only with the right equipment and preparation. Otherwise, the winds may bowl you over.

Please note that I am speaking in terms of energy. It is quite possible to center oneself in spirit and in the sacred in such a way that you walk as a clear and calm eye within the hurricane. But you do not "buffer" a hurricane in the sense of taking it in and trying to transform it or calm it unless you know positively that your energy field can adequately contain it, hold it, and calm it.

Lest this all be too abstract, consider trying to take in to yourself alone all the energy and momentum of pain, suffering, hatred, revenge, fear, and anger generated over many decades, if not centuries, between Jews and Arabs or Protestants and Catholics or Moslems and Hindus (or Moslems and Christians, for that matter). This is not what I mean by world work. This is what I mean by confronting planetary evil, and no one person can do it alone. Powerful thought forms live in and sustain themselves by the energy of these hurricanes of conflict and separation; they feed on the fear and suffering.

What I do mean by world work is intervening in a stormy situation to aid and assist people caught in the storm and bringing the light of the sacred and of our radiant personhood into that storm. Doing this can alleviate the storm and it can deny energy to the hurricane, but it is not the same as confronting the hurricane directly.

However, and this is very important, all acts of love, healing, joy, caring, compassion, skillful assistance, and the like—everything we are discussing as world work—does impact on the hurricanes and lessens their force. It's not that what we do has no effect; it might have a terrific effect. It's just that we achieve that effect not through direct confrontation (though there are beings who do that, too, as I mentioned) but through changing the environment and altering the conditions that allow the hurricane to exist.

Well, I did not mean to get into a rant on psychic protection here. I started out by saying that buffering is a technique that goes beyond world work. It is useful and vital in doing world work, but it is useful in other areas and activities as well as a form of healthy energy management.

There are other inner tools which are also important to world work—and to other activities as well. I think of all of them as making up our "service kit," like a toolkit we take with us into our mindful acts of service. It is this service kit I wish to discuss with you next.

In thinking of this service kit, I have some specific tools in mind. Some of these I am only just going to mention without going into too much detail, but a couple of them are very important to me, so I want to focus upon them.

You may think of other tools. I'm quite sure my list is not exhaustive! Our service kit is very individualized and unique; like a medicine bag that a shaman might wear, it will contain elements useful and meaningful to us.

The tool I want to concentrate on here is Joy: the attunement to and sustaining of Joy.

Joy is one of the most profound, creative, healing, transformative, and powerful forces in the cosmos. It is what the sacred is made of.

Joy is not the same as happiness, though the two are certainly related. Joy is not necessarily the absence of suffering or difficulty.

Joy is not simply an emotion. It is a quality, an energy, a force of life.

As all of us know joy can be experienced in different ways, from a quiet sense of "ok-ness" to a feeling of rapture and bliss. Mostly it is an underlying sense that all is well. It is an attunement to what my friend William Bloom calls the "benevolent field of the universe." I think of it as a surety of God's presence, realizing the underlying sacredness of creation.

Happiness and joy are kissing cousins, obviously. But I think of happiness as an emotion or sensation that is influenced by outcomes. If something works out, I'm happy; it if doesn't I'm unhappy, or at least not happy. But joy is independent of outcomes. Joy is part of the architecture of being, part of the structure of the house, if you will, and thus more than just content within that house.

Joy is an essential part of our service kit because it is a powerful, steadying and transformative energy. Feeling unhappy at the state of the world or at a particular event is natural and may be a realistic and appropriate response to what is going on. But we don't want our energistic field to radiate that unhappiness into the situation, if we are attuning to it. What we want to bring in is a sense of possibilities and energies of transformation, healing, insight, learning, recovery and the like, and all of those are nurtured and empowered by joy.

Even more than love, I believe we need joy, for it seems to me that joy opens the space through into which love can enter.

I've been thinking about joy over the Thanksgiving holiday just past—and about gratefulness as well, both of which seem to me to be part of our Service Kit.

I was trying to come up with an exercise in generating joy, but in conversation with others, I realize (again!) just how uniquely we each engage with these spiritual qualities. What may work for one person may not for another, and we each find our way towards what we need.

I experience joy as a background "buzz" or energy in my life. It is, I believe, the presence of the soul—joy is the vibration or buzz of its presence—and it is also what I think of as the background radiation of creation. This joy does not attach itself to anything; it is more like having an underground stream on one's property into which one can dip when needed.

The issue for us, though, to continue this last metaphor, is to know how to dig down to it. Knowing water is under my feet and actually getting down to it to make a well are two different things. There is something I must do to get to that water.

If I think of that intervening soil and earth as my life's circumstances and the general energy/conditions that surround me as a being upon this earth at this time, then there are times when the soil seems particularly deep and rocky and parched and other times when its thin and moist and easy to dig through. Sometimes, I merely need to turn my attention to the underground river of joy, and it bursts forth. Other times, I seem to need to dig and dig and dig: I must put effort and thought and energy into making the connection. This means that I must be willing to make that effort, willing to seek out the underlying joy of my life. That is a choice.

The effort may require focusing my thoughts, banishing negative feeling and thinking from my mental surrounding, doing something to change my attitude and atmosphere. It may mean using the tools of buffering that we have explored to capture and transform the imagineels of despair and negativity.

But however I do it, I need the water to moisten and vitalize the soil. Nothing new will grow, change will not happen, without that moisture. Joy irrigates my life.

Anyway, as I was saying, I was thinking of what a joy exercise might look like, but given how differently we each may approach this, I am settling for a compromise. If you have a problem finding joy, then I suggest you find someone you know and trust who can help you with this. For this text I will assume that you have a sense of how you can attune to joy and bring its quality into your life when you do world work.

What might be other attributes in your Service Kit? Well, for me they would include gratefulness, a sense of honor and appreciation—and love!—for myself as a specific person, and for my humanity and humanity in general. I find it important to have a sense of the power, the giftedness, the spirituality of humanity as a spiritual presence. This is not to deny the obvious problems we have and which we create as human beings, but it is to have a sense of the value of who we are as a reason not to give up hope and to keep working to bring the best of ourselves into manifestation.

A sense of humor and a sense of perspective are vital to me.

Self-knowledge is always important. In this instance, I want to know what may be present in my emotional and mental field that may prejudice me in doing world work (taking one side or another). I want to know what glamour may exist for me in world work (being a spiritual warrior, fighting for the Light, doing battle with evil: these are the usual and biggest glamours, drawing on our love of drama, but a glamour can also include using world work as a source of meaning and purpose in my life).

One big glamour is an addiction to drama. Particularly in the West, when we think of stories, we think in terms of a specific dramatic arc centered on conflict: The protagonist encounters a problem, there is opposition, there is conflict, the conflict is resolved (usually in favor of the protagonist, unless the story is a tragedy), and there is victory. The overcoming of difficulties is at the core of drama.

But it is not necessarily at the core of life. The dramatic arc is only one way of viewing and understanding life. It is really a form of shorthand, a mythic structure for encapsulating and highlighting dynamic elements, but when you think about it, it is really a very simplistic view of life and events. It tends to paint the world in blacks and whites and actively seeks the energy and stimulus of conflict. It leads us to think of ourselves as protagonists in a drama rather than as complex participants in a holistic cosmos.

The fact is, as a little reflection will show, that life is far more complex than the dramatic structure presents. We are not living our lives as stories nor is all the world a stage with ourselves as actors.

That is a simplified worldview—a kind of "meaning matrix"—that we superimpose on events, often with distorting and sometimes tragic results.

In some modern therapies and self-development approaches, we are encouraged to see our lives as stories, to write out our personal myths, to "tell our stories." This can be helpful in gaining a certain perspective, but from the soul's point of view, I believe it is misleading and even distorting, building in and reinforcing bad habits of thought and perception. If we are living out stories, they are very complex ones indeed, far more complex than the usual "Act I, Act II, Act III" structure we are most familiar with.

It is not that the dramatic arc is wrong so much as it limits our sight; it does not let us see deeply enough or broadly enough. And it can tie us to roles: the hero, the victim, the villain, the innocent bystander, the sidekick, the love interest, and so forth. None of these roles comes anywhere close to defining the true complexity and participation of a human being. While they might be useful at times in analyzing our personality structure or relationships, they are wholly inadequate to even beginning to throw light on the nature and activity of the soul.

In effect, World Work takes place in an energistic environment. In this context, we are working on the inner with subtle forces. It is a different, though complementary, work than doing physical things to help out.

What I want to realize is that I, as a presence of energy and spirit, am entering an environment of energy to effect a change. I am entering an environment in which mental and emotional energies and qualities have a far greater impact than they do on the physical level. It's as if I am a chemical compound being added to a test tube in which other chemicals and chemical reactions are present. I can add to the process or I can trigger an explosive reaction. I need to take care and exercise wisdom and awareness.

The Service Kit is a metaphoric way of talking about the kind of energies and qualities you are going to take with you (embody) to draw upon when you enter into the energistic environment of doing world work. I emphasize joy even more than love or compassion, for example, because it is the quality that prevents you from being caught up in the energies of the problem. It is the deep knowing of the goodness and wholeness of creation, in spite of the immediate problem or the impact of negative energies coming from that problem. It keeps you centered and with a perspective that generates energy and will, not to mention love.

The basic problem of world work as an energistic phenomenon is simple: do I become part of the problem or the solution?

It is the same problem we discussed with buffering. Ideally, we seek to enter a problem situation as the presence and embodiment of the energy to perceive and to act upon a wider selection of options than might have been present before. We are there to expand the playing field upon which or within which the problem will be worked out and resolved.

What does it mean, for example, to send Light to Bush and Saddam to avoid a war? Are we trying to force them along a particular path? Are we altering them in some way? Just what is that Light doing?

In simplest terms, it is opening up a space for both of them within which their own higher natures have a greater chance to operate, in part through gaining a new perspective. The Light we send or impart is heightening the chances that alternative futures or options will open up beyond those that are driven by the forces of habit, hatred, fear, and so on. We are altering the chemical composition of the test tube environment so that a different chemical reaction may occur than might have otherwise. We are acting as a kind of catalyst.

This can be a subtle interaction. If we enter the situation cloaked in the energy of a spiritual warrior, for example, we are carrying a chemistry of conflict ourselves. We have an intent for peace but we carry an energy of conflict. Which will the situation pay attention to? If it is already a situation saturated with energies of conflict, might not our sense of "warriorhood," of drama, of excitement and purpose actually fuel the reaction we don't want?

Joy, on the other hand, as an example, throws a monkey wrench into the process. Why is joy there when the situation is so awful or destructive or filled with hatred? What is there to be joyous about? A question, a puzzlement, an enigma is introduced into the process (metaphorically speaking). Everything pauses, so to speak, to take this new phenomenon into account, and in that pause, it is possible to open to new directions.

Joy, in a way, makes us think beyond the box, beyond habit, beyond the moment. It is a powerful energy for inspiring change.

What other qualities might help to be part of the solution and not part of the problem? What else might you put into your Service Kit?

I want now conclude this Service Kit discussion and start on the actual process of doing world work, taking on some specific events or issues to work with. So the rest of this text will be focused on working on specific techniques.

So far in this text, we have been looking at preparations for world work: the attitudes, attunements, perspectives, and the like that can aid us in engaging with the world.

The assumption here has been that our world work is on behalf of suffering and pain in the world, seeking to bring love and compassion, light and healing to places and situations where these are lacking...or seeking to hold the power of qualities such as peace in situations where such power is needed to provide options for how things may work out.

World work can also be a work of affirmation and support. Our world may seem at times consumed by darkness, but it has plenty of light as well. When we read or hear about positive activities or people who are bringing light, innovation, joy, discovery, creativity and the like into the world, a perfectly appropriate form of world work is to hold them, embrace them, and surround them with energy and a fostering quality. World work need not always or only deal with the shadows!

However, it is the shadows that call out for light and the presence of joy and love. Our service kit, like a doctor's bag, is usually packed with this in mind, that we go to heal.

Notes & Reflections

Chapter Six:
World Work Situations

So how do we begin?

In truth, there is no one best way to answer that question. So much rests upon the individual worker and the nature of the situation. But broadly speaking, there are three kinds of situations upon which we may focus and three kinds of approaches which we may use which we will discuss in the next chapter.

The situations are:

1. The presence of pain and suffering: the negative cloud.
2. The fork in the road: a question of possible direction.
3. Nourishing seeds: upholding the workers of light.

The situation that we choose to focus upon may be clearly one or another of these three, or it may be a combination of two or more of them. (Things are rarely as simple as they look!) There may also be situations that don't fall neatly into any one of these three categories but represent a fourth or fifth possibility. But in the main, in doing world work, we are usually dealing with one of these three.

Let's look at each of these more fully.

The Negative Cloud

By negative cloud, I mean the presence of a psychic force that is obstructive, toxic, and negative in its nature. Think of it as psychic smog! Or think of it as a field of thought and emotion and energy (often made up of fear) that weakens people, diminishes their sense of the light, that is disempowering, and obstructive to positive action, hope, and vision. It is a field that can rob them of their sovereignty.

This "cloud" or "field" may have come into being due to a specific event like a natural disaster. People have been injured and killed. There is suffering and pain. Fear is rampant. Or a social disaster may have occurred: there is upheaval, rioting, even war. Perhaps it is an environmental calamity which is not sudden but which over time drains the capacity of the people involved. This might be like a draught that ruins crops and produces starvation.

I think of a cloud of this nature as resting on the surface of the collective psyche. It is an emergency and there is urgency about the need it represents. But like morning fog, that can be dissipated as the sun rises, this cloud can be diminished as light is brought into it.

A second type of cloud is more tenacious. Like the mist over a fetid swamp, it resists being dispersed. It is not a surface phenomenon alone but is rooted deeply into the collective psyche or even into the earth itself. Healing it means not just blowing away the mists but draining the swamp.

This kind of cloud develops around historical situations, such as long-standing enmities and hatreds between people. It is a cloud of collective human karma, and dealing with it is a human collective responsibility.

This kind of cloud or field is more than an individual can take on as a whole, though an individual can clear away patches of it and deal with an individual "plot" within the swamp. But the healing of such a field depends, paradoxically, upon individuals, since the human collective is made up of persons. So it is not beyond hope or beyond the reach of world work.

In dealing with a cloud, the objective is to bring clarity and light where there is obscuration, fear, and darkness. The challenge is to restore clear sight and clear thought and feeling, to alleviate the energies of pain, suffering, fear, and hatred that cloud people's minds. The power of such a cloud or field is that it subsumes individual sovereignty of soul and becomes a substitute mind that directs the thoughts and feelings of those caught within it, always in a negative way. Or it just makes clear thought and feeling difficult.

The task of the world worker is to lighten this situation in all senses of that word.

In this kind of situation, the world worker is dealing directly with negative energies of various kinds and degrees of power, persistence, and resistance. And if this cloud or field is long lasting and rooted in history, chances are it has developed a form of intelligence as well that primarily focuses upon its own survival and continuation. In short, the energies may have coalesced into a thought-form that now feeds upon the people it affects, stimulating behavior that will maintain its existence.

Later we will look at ways of dealing with such a cloud. What tools would you like in your service kit to deal with this kind of situation?

The Fork in the Road

This is a situation in which choices are being made and options are available and the people involved are determining the direction they will take. The current flare up with Iraq is a good example of this.

This kind of situation may generate its own cloud of thought and feeling or be under the influence of such a cloud. For example, there is a great deal of thought and emotion swirling around the government of the United States that is generated by fears, angers, and the like associated with terrorism, Saddam, war, and so forth. So some kind of "cloud work" may also be necessary.

But here what is needed is open space, wisdom, and clear vision for those who are making the decisions. Information and guidance, intuition and light need to flow to all involved. The role of the world worker on the inner here is to work to create or maintain that open space. It is not necessarily to take sides.

The temptation is to believe we know what the right road to take is. It is entirely possible that what has prompted us into tackling this situation as a form of world work is a spiritual intuition or vision of the best direction, in which case we may have a clear mandate to hold the image of that direction being chosen.

But often we simply work out of our own concerns, preferences, and the like. There is nothing inherently wrong in this. We have every right as sovereign, co-creative beings to let our voice, our minds, and our hearts be heard and seen. But we may lack an intuition of a larger picture. Our vision may be incomplete or faulty or driven by our own fears and antipathies. In which case, to project a particular choice upon a fork-in-the-road situation may only be to add to the "cloud" or the obscuration that the participants must deal with.

So first we are instruments and servants of clarity, then, if need be, and the vision is clear and strong, we can become instruments and servants of a particular direction.

What complicates the issue is that often these fork-in-the-road situations emerge as part of collective karma. We bear a collective responsibility in the choice, but part of the karma is carried specifically by the individuals involved. Life and spirit has brought them to this point of choice for a reason that is both collective and personal. As a world worker, I need to be careful that I don't interfere with this process, even as I stand up to shoulder my own part in the collective karma.

Again, a little later we will look at steps and actions we can take and tools we can use in this situation. But first I have a story to tell.

Up until about a month or so ago, I felt very clearly that I understood the inner dynamics swirling around the Bush Administration, particularly in relationship to Iraq. To me, distinctly negative forces were at work, part of whose aim was the diminishment of freedom in this country and the generation of chaos in the world. I felt that Bush was basically a puppet in the hands of these forces, not because he was aligned with them but because I felt he was energetically empty inside. I felt others in his administration were more directly manipulative of the situation, though, I hasten to clarify, there was no one whom I would identify as a "black magician" or deliberately and directly in league with darker elemental forces.

As part of this vision, I felt that the election had been manipulated and that Gore had truly had the presidency stolen from him.

It is my policy when I have such visions and thoughts to pay attention to them but not to hold them too tightly. I am always open to new and differing information, and look upon any inner vision much as a scientist views a hypothesis. It is something to proceed with in a quest for knowledge and insight, but it must be open to testing as well.

Anyway, around the end of November and the beginning of December, I had a strong, clear vision one morning. I saw Gore and Bush standing near to each other, each on a path that converged on the Presidency, which was represented to me as a circle of light in front of the white house. Gore was in the lead and was about to take the step that would put him into the circle. Suddenly a giant hand stretched down from the heavens, just like the Hand of God, and very gently, very lovingly but very firmly stopped his progress and moved him aside so that Bush had room to pass. Then Bush stepped into the Presidency.

Watching this, I had a powerful sense of the rightness of this. I felt that something had changed or shifted in the world, that something (I don't know what) had changed at a higher level and new possibilities had come into being. In this changed situation, Bush was a better choice to be in that office, was more karmically attuned, than was Gore.

This was an amazing vision! It largely contradicted what I had been feeling before. I found myself forced to reevaluate. The world work I had been doing around Bush and his administration now seemed inappropriate. Something new was needed or being asked of me.

There followed a series of inner experiences and contacts after this experience. None were quite so visionary and explicit, but all pointed in the same direction, which was that Bush was where he was supposed to be and that he was the right person to be there. I found myself in contact with what I think of as a very high level of beings, entities who overlook and guide the destiny of the world as a whole and who seem to reside in what to me is our future. Maintaining contact with them was challenging and the information was hard to hold onto because of the differential between their consciousnesses and my own. Indeed, I felt that actually I was like a child being hoisted on the shoulders of a parent to see a parade better. I felt my usual allies were lifting me up to see at a level of vision that I usual do not attain.

The gist of what I was seeing was that forces were at work which were shaping a new and much better world and which were in fact making use of the energy and nature of the elemental forces I had been perceiving as negative (and which on the whole are negative, at least with respect to human evolution, which they perceive as a threat to their own nature and wellbeing). The possibility of a war in the Middle East I could see from this perspective could be the birth pains of a better world, a drawing out of karmic energies for their resolution, and the using of a strong, negative momentum to actually move the world towards a peaceful and positive future.

In short, I felt I was being told, "don't be so sure what you see and feel is all there is. There is more going on that what you have been aware of, and the choices before you are not necessarily what they seem."

Now, to be clear here, I was not being told that I should choose or work for war with Iraq or North Korea or anywhere, but that I needed to see more deeply past the immediate obvious fork-in-the-road choice between war and peace. Like a vast judo throw or aikido action, a negative momentum was being seized and emphasized, throwing the "adversary" off balance and shifting the leverage and nature of the attack to achieve a higher level of safety and protection. No one said, "do not choose peace". What was being said to me was, sometimes the choice is not between the options that are most apparent.

I am still working with all this, seeking to see more clearly, and to understand more clearly. I have no answers yet out of this experience. I have had more insights into the people whom I previously thought were acting as negative agents within the Administration and am revising my thoughts there too in a more compassionate direction!

The upshot of this is that at the moment, if someone asks me how to do world work around the US-Iraqi situation, I have become more tentative and less willing to just pronounce on the matter. There is mystery here before whose presence I bow, and my first step in world work in this situation is to keep very, very open and to keep my intuition alive and questing.

This is just my own personal experience, and I do not share it as any form of revelation about how things "really" are; I'm not trying to influence your own thinking and feeling. What I want to illustrate is not that Bush is doing the right thing by seeking war with Iraq but that when doing world work, we need to be open to new visions and insights that affect how we work and how we can be of service. We must be careful to discern between personal opinion and desire and the perceptions of our own higher wisdom...and even those perceptions can change by contact with sources with greater vision and knowledge.

One thing I know. If I, or we, approach any situation with a clear desire to bring love and unobstructed wisdom to it, we are unlikely to go far wrong.

Nourishing Seeds

This is a situation in which it seems most appropriate to uphold and empower individuals on the scene who are working to bring resolution, light and betterment to the process. Of course, I could say that this situation also exists as part of the first two I have mentioned, and that would (hopefully!) be true, that whether in a cloud or field of negativity or in a crisis of decision making, there are those present who are attuned to the highest that will serve the largest good and unfold the sacred. And even if there is no identifiable person present (who are the light-workers around Saddam or Kim Jong Il?), the soul within every person is a light-worker and strives to bring the presence of sacredness into the world. Who knows what tiny spark might be touched and ignited in an otherwise unresponsive personality?

However, the kind of situation I have in mind here is one in which there is no urgent crises but a slower, drawn out procedure of change and work to overcome inertia and move the human world towards better states of being. Think, for example, of the long-term work of the United Nations or the work of educators, doctors, and others to effect positive change. Underneath all the flashy events that capture the news, there is a layer of work that is not dramatic but is a steady push towards transformation and healing of the world's ills. It could be as simple and vital as inwardly supporting teachers in the public school system, particularly in inner city schools, that day after day cope with inadequate supplies, scanty pay, challenging kids, and the like in order to motivate our children and help them be participants in creating better lives for themselves and a better world for all of us. They need world work on their behalf as much as the members of the Bush White House or the victims of an earthquake in central Asia or South America.

World work need not be global; it most definitely can be and should be local as well. If a school is in trouble, let it be a focus; if a city is struggling, let it be a focus. And in this kind of work, where there may be no discernable crises but only the drain of slogging against inertia, empowering those who carry the seeds of vision, of light, of love and encouragement is exactly the kind of world work that is needed.

Let's move along here and consider the three approaches I mentioned above (understanding, of course, that these are quite generic and don't in any way cover all the possible ways of doing world work).

Notes & Reflections

Chapter Seven:
World Work Approaches

Three approaches to world work are:

1. You and me, God!
2. Being that which I render.
3. Working with allies.

Of course, in any given situation you may use a combination of two of more of these approaches. And there may be other approaches that you discern may be useful or necessary in a particular situation.

In addition, there are two general tools that I believe are always needed. An Open Intuitive Space is always important. What we see is not always what is there, so leave space for the unperceived and the unexpected. Being unobstructing is also necessary. We want to honor the Intelligence in the situation.

You and me, God

The most familiar form of this way of working is prayer. The simplest form of prayer is supplication, asking the sacred to use its power to make things right in a given situation. Millions of people do this kind of world work everyday just as a matter of course. We pray for peace. We pray for the alleviation of suffering. We pray for the success of beneficial projects and actions. We pray.

Prayer, though, is more than a conversation with the Almighty or a supplication of divine help. Or perhaps I could say, if I'm going to think of it as a conversation, then I need to consider to what depths a conversation may go and the communion to which it may lead.

In fact, let's take that tact for a moment. A conversation may be purely transactional. I come up to you on the street and ask if you could give me a quarter for a parking meter as I am out of change. If you are kindly inclined, you will probably say "Sure," and give me what I need. And that's that. You have given me a quarter and I have given you an opportunity to do a good deed for which you will feel good the rest of the day! End of story.

It is what I call in my book *Blessing: The Art and the Practice* a kindness. In the image I use in that book, no blood and breath is exchanged. There is no sharing of a life force, nor need there be. The situation does not demand it.

Is that the nature of our prayer conversation with God? Are we just asking for a kindness? Are we simply being transactional?

When we pray to God we are usually asking for a blessing. A blessing, though, is not only something one person does for another. It is something that is co-created. A blessing is not imposed as much as it is cooperatively evoked. A blessing is a partnership at work (even though one partner may supply a good deal more of whatever is needed than the other may be able to offer). A blessing draws two or more participants into a shared and generative field.

So a prayer conversation with God is not like simply asking for a quarter for a parking meter. It is something deeper and more involving. It is the creation of a mutual field: "God + Me" or "I + God."

Consider this situation. If I say to you, "Hey, let's go have a cup of coffee," I'm probably not being literal in this request. That is, the purpose is not just to drink caffeine. The purpose is more a social one. I want to be with you, to get to know you, to share some time with you. The conversation we have is not just something we do when our mouths aren't full of coffee, an exercise for the tongue when it's not engaged in tasting and swallowing. The conversation we have is field-building between us. It is a means to achieve a state of mutuality and communion, a sharing of time and life together.

This is putting it all very simply. There are a good many books and techniques out there about how to pray, the meaning of prayer, and the like. But essentially, my take on it is that if I am going to see prayer as a conversation (a big if from a mystical point of view!), then it is a conversation that take us into each other, leading to deeper sharing and communion.

But for myself, I see prayer as a means into the sacred, a way of taking on or realizing the sacred within myself. I suppose here the metaphor of conversation isn't too far fetched, either, since often in conversations of any depth we discover in the other things that are similar to what we find in ourselves.

If I think of prayer as an entering into God, a participation in sacredness, then I can still hold an image of a goal or desire that I would like affirmed and empowered by that participation. But now I am not simply asking for it; I am a participant in its unfoldment. Through my prayer—or my communion—with the sacred, I make that presence more, well, present and operative. I bring the answer fully into the world in which the problem belongs. God, in a way, becomes part of the system in need rather than trying to act upon it from the outside (not such a good metaphor, actually, since the sacred transcends categories like inside and outside, here and there, but still, I hope it conveys the sense of my meaning).

So I see prayer as a form of partnership. God might not need it, but I do, for in prayer I have an opportunity to deepen into my own sacredness, or if I wish to put it another way, I become infused with sacredness, the presence of God. However I put it, as "Me + God" I bring more "soul power" or transformative, loving energy to the situation than I might otherwise. Prayer can deepen me, and from that depth I bring more to my world work.

There are other aspects as well to doing my world work with God, so to speak. If I align myself to the sacred, however, I experience and name that Mystery, I am more likely to approach a given situation in a more loving and neutral way for all concerned. I take a "God's eye view," so to speak. This can be very important. I also am drawing into my life and work the most protective, loving and wise energy there can be. This can't be anything other than a plus in world work!

This is also a very good approach if I don't have a clue what the situation may need. I can ask, in effect, that "God's will be done" or that the "highest manifest for all concerned," or some other equally non-directive intent that is still powerful because it opens my heart and mind, and through my connection with it, potentially the situation itself to energies flowing and actions unfolding that I would not have imagined or been able to foresee or understand.

Here is an important point, though. Using such non-directed prayer does not always mean just leaving it all in God's hands and then walking away (though I grant you there are times when that is exactly what it means and exactly what we should do!). It means doing our inner work to keep the situation clear and unobstructed so that God's will or spirit or presence can manifest in natural and organic ways. The latter is important to my point of view. No one likes an imposed situation, and it is unlikely to prove long-lasting. But if the answer emerges from within and thus seems integral and organic to the situation and the people involved, then it can "stick." (This to me is why God works from within: it looks like we're doing it ourselves!) <grin>

Leaving it in God's hands, then, is not the same thing as abandoning our own work. "Oh well, good ol' God will take care of it!" This is not the best option! Our love and attention are still important ingredients in creating the field that ultimately lets God "do it."

Ok, at this point I would like you to do some reflection. What do you think about what I've been saying so far about prayer, God, and the partnership between you (as well as the beingness you share)? Do you have experiences that come to mind? Do you have insights to add? What does prayer mean to you? How might you or how do you use prayer in world work? Obviously, this particular discussion is very biased towards a theistic approach, one that accepts the existence of God or the sacred as an active presence in creation. But one doesn't have to use the idea of God. One can substitute the idea of the Tao or of natural law or the ground of all being. The point in this approach is that I am aligning myself with something that is universal and shared by all in one way or another.

Being that which I render

In the first general approach to world work, we do so by aligning with the sacred within ourselves and within the world, God immanent and transcendent, however we may define or experience that.

In the second approach, we are drawing on our own self, our own inner being or incarnational character and presence. In this instance we bring to the situation whatever wisdom, love, peacefulness, compassion, courage, and the like that we find within ourselves. In so doing, we exercise both these qualities and, like a muscle, our capacity to experience and hold these qualities in the midst of all that transpires around us in the course of our day...or in the midst of whatever images, energies, sensations, thoughts, and feelings may arise when we attune to or meditate upon a particular situation.

At a deeper level, though, we become mediators—inductors, if you will—of the quality or qualities we wish to bring into a situation or to a person. We inhabit that quality or those qualities and we make them available by virtue of being them in the moment. We are that which we would render unto the situation.

In this approach, I am not drawing a quality to me from the outside, as I might do when working with my images of and contact with the sacred. The sensation or felt sense is more that of drawing it up from my own personal inner resources. Or maybe, rather than think of myself as sharing a cloak of qualities with God, I am donning my own cloak of those qualities from my own closet!

However one imagines this, the issue is that I come to the situation standing in the power of that quality which I intend to share.

This means I approach the world work slightly differently. (By the way, I hope it's understood that these three approaches are not exclusive. In actual fact, we may use elements of all three. Though I stand in my own quality of peace, for example, there is no reason I cannot also draw on the peace of the sacred or invoke the sacred or draw upon the presence and energy of allies. I separate these three primarily to highlight each of them.)

Instead of beginning with a meditation or prayer or attunement to the sacred (though, as I say, one can do that as well), I begin by attuning to the quality or qualities I wish to embody. I use whatever means I wish to do this. I could use imagination, visualizations, movement, music, pictures...whatever allows that quality to arise and live in me. And as it arises, I immerse myself in it, as if taking a bath in it.

When I feel ready for my world work, then I attune to or meditate upon the situation and bring it into my field which is saturated with this quality (as much as I am able) or I step imaginally into the situation carrying this quality with me.

That is the general principle. Thinking about it, I am reminded of Emerson's saying that "what you are speaks so loudly I cannot hear what you say." It is an analogous situation.

I already wrote earlier when talking about our tool kit about the importance of joy, which I experience not simply as happiness but as a sense of connection with what my friend William Bloom calls the "blissfield" of creation. Joy is what I think of as an "opening" or "unobstructing" quality, and I think of it as the base upon which I anchor other qualities with which I may wish to work. Rather like the undercoat I put on a wall when painting before applying the actual colored paint I wish to use.

If prayer is the generic exercise for working with God, then contemplation or reflective meditation would probably be the equivalent here. I contemplate the quality I wish to take on.

Contemplation is a discipline about which much has been written in a context of Christian mysticism and spiritual practice. As I practice it, it goes something like this (but feel free to adapt this to your own personal nature). I call this technique the Three Thinkings: Thinking About, Thinking Into, and Thinking With.

Thinking About

Let's say I want to bring peace into a situation. I begin by thinking about peace as an idea, as an emotion, as a felt sense in my body. What does peace mean to me, for instance? What is peace? Is it only the absence of conflict? How do I experience it? And so on. I am forming my thoughts and my feelings about peace.

In this step I am turning my thoughts towards peace as an idea and as an experience and away from other thoughts. I am giving peace my attention.

I think of this step as getting to the right address. I am turning my thoughts and attention to where peace lives, so to speak, so I can pay it a visit.

This step need not be very long. With practice I can go through it very quickly. After all, I'm not trying to prepare a dissertation on the meaning of peace! I'm only trying to align and attune myself mentally and emotionally to the quality of peace, both as it manifests specifically in my personal life and experience and as a larger quality in the world.

Thinking Into

In this step, I am using thought and feeling, largely in the form of imagination, to go into the essence of peace. If the thought or image of peace is like a seed pod, in this step I am breaking it open to get at the nut within.

Please note that I am not trying to come up with the definition of peace or the essential nature of peace in any mental or discursive way. That would be thinking about it. Here I am actually moving away from concepts of peace into the energy and presence of the quality itself.

If the first stage was getting to the right address, in this stage I'm entering the house and meeting its inhabitant. Just as I am not defined wholly by my address or by the house in which I live, the forms that surround me, so peace is not defined by any single thought or combination of thoughts about it. Peace is a living presence, an energy if you will, and in this stage I am sinking (thinking) into it.

The use of thought here is to hold the image, to hold a particular form of peace that I have come to through Thinking About so that that image or form is a portal into experiencing peace. I am engaging with the life of peace, the living presence of peace, and forming a relationship and a union with it.

Here I am using my imagination to become peace, to feel its presence as my presence, or to feel it organically and naturally unfolding from my presence. My experience of this stage is that of the quality, in this case peace, rising about me and filling my field, becoming the presence in which I move and have my being. I am inhabiting the space where peace dwells.

This is a stage of immersion.

Thinking With

This is the deepest stage or perhaps I should say the most fully realized stage. This is when peace, in this instance, ceases to be an image or thought outside of me and becomes me. Now peace is not a thought I think about but a thought I think with, a formative thought.

Having found the right address and entered the house, I now have married the inhabitant so that it has become my house, too. This is the stage of contemplative union with whatever quality or attribute I am working with.

Indeed, though I call it "thinking with," in fact I have most likely passed beyond thought here and entered a space of being and knowing.

I am one with the quality just as I am one with myself. I am being that which I wish to render.

These three stages, the Three Thinkings, are more suggestions about the contemplative process then rigid prescriptions. One can incorporate elements of prayer, movement, music, dance, ritual, and the like to aid the contemplative process. You may find yourself going through four stages or even five, or you may go directly from your everyday mind into Thinking With (which actually is likely if you have some practice and experience in contemplative work).

Notes & Reflections

Exercise Six:
The Three Thinkings

I have written earlier a description of this exercise and an example of how I use it. Here, I have two parts to this exercise for you to do.

Part 1

In the first part, I would like you to pick a quality and contemplate it going through the steps of the Three Thinkings. I want you to Think About the quality you have chosen, Think Into it, and Think With it. I would like you to pay attention to any differences you feel between these three stages and to anything that arises for you in each stage.

Part 2

This process may not be the most natural for you. It follows a sequence of thinking, imagining, being, but your sequence might be different. In this second part, I want you to reflect on the technique itself, in the sense of paying attention to how it fits your mode of working. If you do something different or would naturally prefer to contemplate in a different way, what is your alternative way?

Note that the object of this second part of the exercise is not to critique the technique of the Three Thinkings as much as it is to use the technique as a way of perceiving your own way of moving into being that which you render, assuming that you may wish or need to do it a different way.

Notes & Reflections

So, if the technique is useful to you and works for you, why is this so? What do you learn about yourself? And if it is not so useful and doesn't work so well, why is this so? Again, what do you learn about yourself and how you contemplate?

And it may be that your way into beingness has nothing to do with contemplation at all!

Anyway, try the exercise, do the Three Thinkings, and reflect on the process, all as a way of illuminating an answer to the question, "How do you become and be that which you wish to render or offer in the course of your World Work."

Now, here are some further thoughts about this.

I am writing about this as if we become the quality we wish to render in a singular way, that is, as if we are that quality and nothing else.

Such one-pointed concentration is certainly possible. But is it desirable?

Well, it certainly achieves clarity and focus when such concentration is there, and in fact, angels of qualities do embody such purity of presentation. But a human being is not that kind of an angel. We are not the highly refined and pure chemical itself but a retort in which chemicals are mixed and alchemies performed. We are chemistry, not a chemical.

We are where qualities come to express themselves in unexpected and novel ways.

Thus, while I can immerse myself in a quality such as peace or courage, love or compassion, it is not so much an act of simplifying myself but of "complexifying" the quality. The quality becomes a strange attractor around which a complex field may develop. It is the major theme we bring to a situation, but it may inspire variations.

A pure quality, from a magical or energistic viewpoint, has a will and a logic behind it that is hard to resist but which can be inflexible. We rarely encounter pure qualities at work in the world, though they are certainly at work in the foundations of the world. One reason is that the mixing of qualities and energies creates a more adaptive and dynamic situation, capable of permutations and manifestations that the pure quality by itself might not be able to achieve.

Think of how much would be missing from the world if we could only use (or see) the primary colors. Hues, shadings, nuances, tones would all be absent or unrecognizable. When you think of the beauty and richness of the world, not to mention all the hues of colors that human beings are developing, it is due to the capacity of these pure qualities or primary colors to mix and blend and express in a multitude of specific and individual ways.

So when you contemplate a quality (or use some other method to become a quality), what you are actually becoming is you plus that quality. You are becoming a unique hue or shade of that quality.

Going back to my example above, I am still Peace but I am a David Spangler-version or shade of Peace.

This may seem obvious, but it is very important from a magical sense. Our power as human beings lies in our impurity, so to speak, rather than our purity; that is, in our capacity to be a mix of many things (hopefully in harmony, cohesion, and wholeness) rather than just one thing. A mistake that is sometimes made in magical or energistic work is to try to become the pure energy, the archetype, the God- or Goddess-form as that presence exists in its own natural environment. I want to be purely love or purely peace. But this can be overwhelming, and it can bind a human being whose nature is to be a synthesis of many things not a purity of one thing. As I said, we are not the pure chemicals but the retort in which they are mixed so powerful and creative reactions can take place.

Operationally, this means that even as I take on the power and strength of a quality, giving it focus and presence within me, I am also aware of myself as an interpreter of that quality. I have the capacity to improvise and to be that quality in ways that are specifically appropriate to a particular condition and in ways that can change and adapt as a situation changes.

So, going back to the Three Thinkings, a fuller exposition of this exercise would be to call it Three Thinkings and a Context. The context is the unique individual life of the person who is invoking and embodying the quality.

If several people embody Peace, do we all do it the same way? Is it the same Peace?

What I bring to the mix—what we each bring to the mix—is also important and gives suppleness and adaptability to the pure but somewhat energistically rigid nature of the quality itself.

In effect, we seek to incarnate the quality, not be possessed by it, and in so doing, it will become David (or whatever your name is) As Peace or Peace as David (or you): David-Peace, Person-Peace.

There is more to this issue of the blending and of incarnating a pure quality into a world of mixtures and combinations.

Consider that when we think of Peace, one of the ways we define it or form a thought about it is often to compare it to its absence or its opposite. We create a polarity. So, for instance, we have Peace and Conflict or Peace and War (unless you're a Russian writer, in which case you have War and Peace).

If I am determined to only be Peace as a pure quality, then might I not be forced into an adversarial stance relative to any other quality or condition I might posit as a polarity to Peace? By being Peace, might I not become in conflict with Conflict?

Is it possible that there is Peace in Conflict, or Conflict in Peace? Is Conflict actually a permutation of Peace, or vice versa?

Standing in my image of the pure quality of Peace, I might say unequivocally, "All Conflict is wrong." But is it?

Which brings me to a final point. How accurate is my sensing or thinking about the nature of a particular quality such as peace? If my images are formed in relationship to conflict, such as "peace is the absence of conflict," am I really attuning to Peace as a quality? Is that all Peace is, or is it something else?

The Three Thinkings can take us deeply into a quality or they can take us deeply into sensations aroused by our image or understanding of that quality. There is a difference, though energistically the latter can feel quite powerful and can be used effectively in world work.

The question here is, do I really understand or can I really experience the pure nature of any quality that fundamentally arises and exists on a level of life and being far different from the one I experience everyday in the world. It may be that the energy of Peace I strive for and experience in meditation is already a mix, not the pure thing after all but a particular manifestation arising within the World Soul or the Soul of Humanity that is accessible to me.

I don't want to get too abstract here or too speculative. For myself, when I attune to a quality that seems to me part of and emanating from the sacred, it is pure enough in its relationship to me and the world as to make no practical difference in world work. It may be as I expand my capacities of perception and awareness I will come to recognize and understand aspects of Peace (or any other quality) that are different and even more "pure" than anything I can experience now. But I am not there yet. The quality I do attune to is plenty pure for my immediate purposes!

The issue I want us to consider here, though, is not the purity of the energy or quality but its incarnational mixing within us and the importance of our unique personhood in this process. I can be peace in order to render it to a situation, and that peace will be more pure than just my thoughts and opinions about peace or even my desires and imaginations about how peace should manifest...but that quality is still living in and acting through me.

If I want my "beingness of peace" or my alchemical elixir of peace to be as pure and powerful as I can make it, then the answer is not just to try to get ever more refined and more pure chemicals but to refine and improve the retort that is my personhood.

So becoming peace is not just a magical operation of taking on and expressing an archetypal or divine quality. It is also working alchemically and transformatively with the material of my personality so that I find myself, my unique incarnational self, as peace—the peace that I am that can connect and blend with the peace that is a pure quality at the foundation of the world.

Who or what am I as peace, not as an archetypal quality but as an ingredient in my own unique incarnational beingness?

For clarification I should say that here I am thinking like a chemist: that chemicals come in "pure" states, that is, states undiluted or uncontaminated by something else. I remember the protocols we had to use in chemical lab to ensure that this purity was safeguarded.

When I think of inner plane qualities, I think like a chemist. These qualities are not psychological to me; they are not even thoughts or feelings per se. They are energies or substances. What I think of as "peace" or "love" or "courage" are the humanly understood manifestations of these "purer" substances or energies, already mixed by passage into and blending with the capacities and energies of the earth.

So, I do think of "peace," in this instance, existing in various states of manifestation stemming from a state that, relatively speaking, is more pure. For me this purity is not the same as the Platonic idea of an ideal form. It is purity in the chemical sense. Of course, one has to go to the sacred itself to find the most pure expression of anything, pure in the sense of virginal and not yet having interacted with any other aspect of creation.

But in my own experience, I touch on the energies or states of qualities that move at a higher level (what I think of in my own cosmology as a stellar or cosmic level, which is about as high as I usually am able to go...there are levels beyond that) and they feel qualitatively different, more refined. I also note that they do not directly interact with the human level but they are the roots of the qualities that do interact with us.

Please note here that the pure form of a chemical may not be its most potent expression. The pure forms of sodium and chloride are poisonous to us, but combined they create salt which enables our kind of life to exist. Similarly for hydrogen and oxygen, which create water. So peace as we know it is already a compound, rather than a pure element, and it becomes further compounded in us. In so doing, it loses its chemical "purity" but it gains potency and capabilities it might not have had in that pure state.

I hope this clarifies my position. I forget sometimes just how much I think out of a chemical or biological paradigm when thinking and speaking about the inner worlds. My approach really isn't that of a philosopher or mystic in many ways, it is that of an alchemist! So I use terms that mean one thing in one context but which have other, undesired meanings in another.

To reiterate, a pure quality to me is not a Platonic ideal but it is an essence that makes other things possible. It is not a closed system in the same way that most elements are not closed systems, except for the inert elements which have their own unique characteristics and uses. But, and this is important, like the inert gases, the presence of a closed system or a fixed system is often necessary and vital to the capacity of an open system to form and exist. It is the relationship of fixed to fluid.

Notes & Reflections

Chapter Eight:
Working with Allies

In this section, I am assuming the hypothesis that there are other realms of being where dwell non-physical persons, both human and non-human (angels, animal powers, etc.), who can act with us as allies, enhancing our capacities for doing world work.

I am not going to spend much time on how to contact allies—that is really another class altogether. I am going to assume that you already either know how to do this or have allies with whom you regularly (or irregularly) work. Contacting allies is not necessary for world work. It is not an approach that everyone will use. But many folks do work with allies, so I wished to include it here.

Actually, when we think of an ally here, we could reasonably think of God or of a quality as an ally, particularly if I think of qualities as being represented by angelic beings (the Angel of Peace, the Angel of Courage, and so forth). In that context, contacting an ally can be as simple as prayer. Millions of Catholics do it all the time when they seek out the intercession of saints. If I pray to Mary or to St. Christopher, for example, I am not praying to God and I am not invoking or becoming a quality, but I am seeking assistance. I am seeking a relationship with a source that I feel can augment my capacities or fill in or act where I am not capable of doing so. I seek an ally because, in part at least, I am seeking the particular characteristics and capacities that that ally represents.

This is similar to invoking a quality, but usually working with an ally is less about being something and more about doing something. That is, they are not allies in beingness but in activity and accomplishment. They are allies in making something happen. I realize this is a distinction that does not always hold up: in the spiritual worlds, being and doing are deeply intertwined. But I make it in order to highlight the particular effect that an ally may have.

An ally is someone who brings his or her or its own capacities, qualities, connections, and the like to bear on a situation in cooperation with myself, often at my invitation.

Popularly, I believe the idea of working with allies is often understood as contacting someone or something that can act in places or in ways that I cannot. It comes close to (and at times, I'm sure crosses over) the line of asking the ally to do it for us or of seeing the ally as someone who will do it for us.

This misses an important point. What we are looking at here in this approach is the power of relational energy. It is a variant of what Jesus said when he said, "Where two or more are gathered in my name, there I am also."

This is such a fundamental algorithm of spiritual work. It is the power of Gathering. But not just any gathering. It is not just a collection that works by accumulation or addition. It is not that two or three or four people are better than one person at accomplishing something; often they are not. It is the "in my name" part that is also important.

I do not imply here the Christian viewpoint that Jesus' name specifically is important (though of course it has its own unique spiritual power). The idea of "Name" in this context means purpose or presence to me; it is a recognition of an organizing principle, the "strange attractor" that enables a living system to come into being. And that living system is more than the sum of its parts. It is an emergent phenomenon, bringing into play capacities that are not present in or are different from the capacities in the individual elements that are doing the gathering.

A smoothly running team, in sports or in business, is a good example of this Gathering. When the organizing or cohering or defining spirit and intent are present, then the power of the gathering is increased exponentially.

In a team everyone contributes. They may not all contribute equally, but all are equal in the act and spirit of contribution. On a team I have allies—my team members—but if I just sit back and let them do it all, then I am not really part of the team. I do not have a team. I do not have an alliance.

When thinking of allies, I am really thinking of alliance. An alliance has allies. But an alliance is more than just having allies. An alliance is a co-created venture; like a team, everyone contributes. I must do something, give something, to create an alliance. It is an active relationship, not a dependent, passive one. The alliance is the body of the Gathering, the emergent spirit which is what the alliance truly wants to manifest and bring into action in the world.

So, in working with allies, I am actually working with the process of gathering and alliance. Obviously this can be done perfectly well with other physical persons like myself, which is one reason group work in which the spirit of gathering and alliance can be fostered and sustained is so powerful. When I seek allies of a non-physical nature, what I am seeking is alliance with qualities and energies, perspectives and insights embodied in particular entities which are not readily available, if at all, to physical persons. I am constrained in various ways by being a physical being in a physical world, but some of those constraints do not apply to non-physical beings (or, for that matter, to our own soul or other non-physical aspects). For example, distance is not the same barrier for an inner plane ally as it can be for me.

But more than the particular skills or capacities such a being might bring, it is the act of forming alliance that is the real effective power here. Something is released through this act that is more than the inner plane being or I could normally invoke or express on our own.

This being the case, what I bring to this alliance is very important. It is why I cannot or should not think of working with allies as simply turning things over to someone else to take care of. That is delegation, not alliance. Not that there can't be a role for delegation, but it is not the same as working with an ally through gathering and alliance.

So, as in the other two approaches, we come back to a common foundation: the importance of the character and role of ourselves as sovereign, unique, individual incarnate persons. That is part of the nub of incarnational spirituality. There is a spiritual power inherent in being ourselves in engagement and relationship with the world as incarnate beings, as distinct personal beings. It is a co-creative, emergent, gathering power.

Exercise Seven:
Prayer "recipe"

I suppose the prayer "recipe" would go something like this (with the understanding that, like any recipe, a good cook will alter it to fit her or his style):

Make personal connection with spirit of the sacred, as you understand and experience it.

Take a moment to commune with that presence, allow it to fill you, allowing yourself to enter and merge with it. You want a felt sense of "me + sacred."

In that space of "me + sacred" or shared presence with the sacred, hold your image of the situation or person for which or for whom you are praying. Hold as well your own response to that situation, the feelings and thoughts it arouses in you. In this sense you are holding both the situation as it is (or more probably as it appears to you as mediated through the filters of the media) and as it is as an image within you.

When these two images are held in the presence, the intent is to deal with both. On the one hand, I want the presence to address the needs of the actual situation, at least insofar as I can define that situation. But I also want and need the sacred to heal or address the situation as it lives in me. The image I hold of the situation, such as the potential of war with Iraq, gathers its own energy around it which may contain my own fears, angers, distress, and so forth. I want my image of the situation made clear and accurate and healed if need be, as much as I want the actual situation to be dealt with. The situation in this sense as it lives in me as an image acts as a portal into my own stuff which may need surfacing, balancing, and healing.

So there are two levels of healing that go on here or two levels of world work: work for the world and work for the world in me.

In the space of "me + God" hold a sense of what you wish for this situation. What in your estimation would help resolve it, both in the world and in your own heart. I don't mean thinking of and holding a full strategy of what should be done, but something more basic and generic.

For example, if I am holding the situation between Iraq and the United States, I'm not holding in mind the strategies that Bush and his administration should be taking in my estimation. I am holding in mind my desire for peace and for wellbeing to be given to everyone involved. I want this situation to be an evolutionary driver for humanity, that out of it comes not only peace but also wisdom and lessons and unfoldment for the participants and for all nations and peoples.

In effect, I am presenting to God my perspective and opinions as a partner. I am not saying "God, this is what you must do," but I am offering my point of view.

Then I enter into silence and allow a response to flow into me from the sacred. This response might be a sense of love or a sense of peace; it might actually be an image. I might have an image, for example, of Secretary of State Powell going to Iraq and meeting with Saddam. I might have an image of a delegation of Arab leaders going to Iraq to mediate with Saddam. Who knows what the image may be? (and there may not be any images either.)

Then, if there is a response, I hold that in the presence of the sacred and offer it to the world as a contribution, a seed thought or image around which activity or inspiration can constellate. If there is no response, then I offer my love and my sense of the presence of the sacred to the situation for its highest good. As you say, I feel that presence being active in the situation.

Finally, I give thanks.

Notes & Reflections

Exercise Eight:
Analyzing and Intuiting a Situation

This exercise is about analyzing and intuiting a situation so you know more clearly what you will be dealing with.

Pick a world situation that holds your attention at this time. It could be the threat of war with Iraq, the Korean crisis, an environmental issue, people in government, whatever you wish.

Imagine this situation spread out before you. Is it clearly one of the three generic situations mentioned in the text? Is it a negative cloud, a fork in the road, or seeds that need nourishing? Is it a combination of these? Do you see other elements present that are not one of these three? If it is a cloud or field of negativity, is it a surface one or does it have roots in the long past? Is it hovering over a swamp, so to speak? If the latter, what do you feel are the deeper energies involved that arise out of the long past?

In short, tune into the situation you have chosen and give us your own analysis and intuition about this situation.

If it is a situation that combines two or more of the three elements mentioned, do you intend to work with the whole combination or with one of the elements within it? Which one?

What about this situation might give you pause to look more deeply and to enter an open intuitive space? What might be there that is not obvious or immediately apparent? Is there something deeper at work here that you might sense?

Notes & Reflections

Chapter Nine:
Collective World Work

Here I want to share my perspective on one way of working with large outpourings of collective energy.

To some extent, this is an issue of style and focus. Some people respond well to and work well with such mass expressions of energy, and others prefer to work with smaller, more precise applications of energy. I happen to be one of the latter for the most part.

I think of trying to open a safe in order to release a stuck energy. Gathering hundreds or thousands or millions of people to concentrate on that safe is akin to releasing a wall of water upon it. It may move the safe, but it probably will not unlock it. However, the sensitive fingers of one person spinning the lock and listening attentively to the tumblers as they move can unlock the safe. Precision often accomplishes what sheer mass and volume cannot.

There is the tendency with large gatherings to think in terms of numbers, as if the amount of people meditating or praying or raising energy had a direct relationship to the quality of the energy itself. On the other hand, there is a power when a collective field is generated, and knowing that a million or more minds are focusing upon a single quality or objective can itself be transformative. It certainly makes a statement that the world can hear and see.

Of course, it is not an either/or situation. The ideal is for each of us to tap into the collective field and give it a precise focus through our own individual lives. There is no use at all in becoming a mob, even a mob for peace; the results can turn in directions we would not want.

When energy is generated but then has no specific outlet through which to ground itself, it can lose its quality and just become a force. An energy of peacefulness just sent out into the world but not grounded can, in my understanding, lose its quality of peacefulness, for example, and then exist as a presence of energy. That energy can be applied then to peaceful purposes or it can be applied just as well to war-making purposes. War can potentially be precipitated energetically by dumping a lot of energy into a situation ill-prepared to integrate and use it, even if that energy is raised in the name of peace.

But there is a lot of use in non-violently and purposefully holding an energy of peace which everyone can attune to and use in acts of peace-making in their daily lives like coming together to raise an energy that can charge everyone's batteries in making peace.

This grounding and direction of a collectively-raised energy takes place in our individual lives through our actions and through our projections of thought and feeling into the world.

So, if you are so inclined—and obviously this must be by personal choice and desire—I would recommend something like the following in order to participate in a mass event.

Three or four days before the event, begin to make peace a focus in your prayer life, contemplative life, spiritual life, etc. Find ways of bringing the quality of peace into your encounters, ways of thinking about peace, ways of embodying peace in your daily activities, etc. As a consciousness, deliberate choice, engage with the spirit of peace and begin to marinate in its qualities.

Explore the nature of that spirit of peace as broadly and deeply as you can, just as you would if this were a person whom you loved deeply and with whom you are starting an intimate and co-creative relationship.

Live with peace, not as an antidote to the world's ills, but as a joyful, playful, profound presence, friend, and companion.

Then on the day, take part in this great mass event just as if the two of you—you and the spirit of peace—were going to a wonderful party. Take part in the event as much as you wish, in whatever way you wish. Celebrate it, just as if it were your friend's birthday or a day when your friend, the spirit of peace, is being especially honored and feted.

During this day, much energy may be raised. There is a difference between energy and the spirit of peace; the latter can manifest the former but the former does not necessarily manifest the latter. When many people are concentrating together, it is energy that may result but not necessarily the deeper quality and presence that one may desire—in a way, the energy can get in the way of the quality.

Have you ever gone to a birthday party or a party of any kind where everyone got high and there was lots of energy, but somehow the deeper qualities of what you were celebrating got lost? Think of a New

111

Year's party in which one celebrates the New Year with shouting and fireworks and singing, but the deeper, reflective quality of that threshold moment is lost. Qualities and energies are not necessarily the same thing!

So as you celebrate on the day, make a special effort or give special attention to linking the two together, linking the energy that is raised by all the thousands and hopefully millions of people with the actual quality of peace. The energy is exterior, in a way, but the quality is interior. What bridges between the two? That is your task on the day, to be that bridge, to integrate in your lives the energy AND the quality of peace, giving peace an energy to work with and the energy a depth and quality of peacemaking and peacefulness.

In part this is done by claiming the spirit of peace as one's own and inhabiting it in one's life and encounters, which is the rhythm you have already established by your work in the days prior to the actual event. Your work leading up to this event prepares your life to absorb this quality and energy. You have already prepared a place in your life to integrate and ground peace.

Thus you do not find yourself on the day generating or experiencing a great outpouring of energy but with no inner preparation to receive and integrate it, anchoring it into the collective body of humanity through your own beingness.

On the following day and for a least seven days thereafter, continue this process. The task here is to absorb and integrate a great "cloud" of energy that has been generated. Angelic and other subtle forces will be doing the same thing. But this energy will not enter the human collective except through human beings. And this is a piece of work. It requires diligence and attention, choice and discipline. Peacemaking is not a one-night stand!

Now you are building and integrating even more your relationship with peace. If you want to use this metaphor, you could say that your peace work leading up to the event is like a courtship, the actual day is the marriage, and afterwards comes the honeymoon and the work of establishing and building the marriage as a solid, joint field.

So each day for at least a week after the event, think and feel into that cloud of energy released that day, link the energy with the quality of peace that you have been already developing and inhabiting for the days before the 9th, and blend the two in the alchemical retort of your own life.

Live peace, inhabit peace, be peace. Make it a natural, organic part of you. Ground it, ground it, ground it through your daily actions and encounters. Then this energy generated earlier has someplace to go, someplace to live, someplace to be fulfilled and will not just hover, where, as energy (no matter what name we give to it), it can be appropriated and utilized by any force willing to ground it.

How many times has the cry and call for peace been turned into a justification for war? Even more to the point, as ever healer knows, if energy is raised and then not grounded, it can burden the body and stimulate the surfacing of difficult toxic material.

What is not well-understood is that the invocation of peace as an energy—the raising of an energy—can precipitate the very war, the very conflict, the very appearance of toxicity that folks want to avoid. It is energetically possible for the peacemaker to ultimately be his or her own worse enemy, the stimulus to the war he or she ardently wishes to avoid. This happens when energy is raised but not well integrated and grounded in the aftermath.

It is also possible that in a larger view of things, the road to a lasting peace may wind through a valley of toxicity and darkness before coming to resolution and healing, just as a patient using natural healing methods can encounter a healing crisis which makes the illness temporarily worse. This can be even more likely if the healer is simply pumping energy into the ill body and stimulating it in a way that the illness is also stimulated and increased.

A hint here: how many peacemakers carry violence in their hearts towards those who would make war or for whom war is a profession? Can not our buried thoughts of adversariality distort and misdirect the energy we raise with all good intentions? How can I integrate and ground peace if my attraction to peace is in opposition to, fear of, and even hatred of those who wish to wage war?

But if a healing crisis is skillfully managed so that healing energy is well-integrated into the patient's own healing powers, then that crisis may past swiftly with little hardship on the road to healing.

Likewise, should a conflict be precipitated by the energies raised for peace so that toxic material in the human unconsciousness can be surfaced and transmuted, if the peacemaking is well integrated in the life of human beings and is not just an energy set loose upon the world, that conflict can turn from something major with much destruction and suffering to something relatively minor that is swiftly resolved.

The key is our ability to claim, own, inhabit and integrate the quality of peace with the energy we generate in the context of our own lives as representatives of humanity. Make this our discipline for at least seven days after the day and the chances of success at global peacemaking are greatly increased.

Of course, the ideal is to continue with this integration and living out of peace for all our days to come.

Notes & Reflections

Chapter Ten:
Doing World Work

The main point I have wished to make in this text is that World Work is an organic outgrowth from how we are incarnationally in the world. It is a specific kind of inner action in which we link our energy with that of a particular situation to give aid, comfort, blessing, and the possibility of transformation. We may specifically invoke and heighten the presence of certain qualities and spiritual energies that we may not normally experience in our everyday lives. But on the whole, the work builds on and expresses seeds and foundations that are already there within us.

So the nature and depth of compassion, love, listening, goodwill, openness, blessing, healing, etc., that I bring into my normal everyday life will definitely affect what I can bring into my world work. When I enter into world work, it's not as if I cross a threshold and become someone else or gain superpowers, like Superman coming out of a phone booth. If I don't have those superpowers when I enter the phone booth, I'm not likely to have them when I leave!

There are exceptions to this rule, and they almost always have to do with the sacred and with allies. Through prayer and through my connection with spiritual allies, I may well be able to bring to bear upon a situation spiritual forces and qualities that I may not be able to summon in the course of my everyday affairs. But even then, my capacity to pray effectively and to link with allies effectively is still conditioned by my overall quality of spiritual life in my normal everyday context.

So the first step in World Work is to realize that everything I do is world work. There is never a time when I am not world working in some fashion, or at least gathering and refining the inner and outer resources that I will bring into my world work.

There is another way we can look at this. When I am formally doing world work, I am engaging with some needful situation and I'm being open to being a means to bring some quality, presence or energy into that situation. Think of it as engaging with aid workers who are carrying and distributing supplies to help victims of some calamity.

The calamity intensifies the need and heightens it, but what meets the need are everyday things the duplicates or the analogs of which we have around the house. So, for instance, an aid worker may supply food, water, medicine, blankets, and clothing to victims in need. But I have food, water, medicines, blankets, and clothing in my house. These are not, in themselves, exotic or unusual items. It is the way in which they may be used and the intensity of the situation within which they are used that makes a difference.

If I make myself familiar with food, water, blankets, clothes, and medicines, which I can do in my ordinary life, then I carry that familiarity with me into the more intense situation and it supports me in what I need to do.

Or let me put it another way. Diplomats gather to try to snatch peace from the jaws of war in Iraq (and who knows, perhaps soon with North Korea as well). The situation is intense because if they are unsuccessful, people will begin to die. Now imagine you are having an argument with a family member; there is anger between you and the possibility of heightened emotional conflict. You are trying to come to a peaceful resolution of your disagreement. Are these two different situations? Is the peace different in one case than in the other case? Certainly the stakes are different; if you fail, no one is going to die (although police statistics show that the number one cause of murders is domestic violence, usually between spouses). But the quality of peace is the same. From one vantage point, you and the diplomats are both doing the same thing, you are engaged with the same issue.

Now, suppose you have failed to find peace with your family member but you enter into world work to send the quality of peace to the diplomats. Is your power to do so as integrated and present as it might have been if you had been successful in creating peace with your family member (or with your boss, or employee, or the waiter who made a mistake in your order, or whomever you may have had an energy of conflict with)?

In our everyday lives, we encounter the same qualities and situations that we will encounter in world work, except that in the latter we encounter them in a more intense and heightened manner generally speaking.

On the other hand, when I do an inner World Work, I want, if possible, to remove my self from my everyday life. I do want to enter a phone booth and become Superman or Superwoman. I want to take on a heightened identity appropriate to the World Work I wish to perform.

In inner world work, I am generating (both within myself and in relationship to allies and the sacred) specific spiritual and magical energies or forces which become the carriers of the qualities I wish to manifest in that situation. This requires coherency, focus, concentration, though not necessarily in a fierce, tune-everything-else-out kind of way. It requires attention.

It also requires deep listening as part of that attentiveness. Unless I am just going to work in a surface way with the situation, I want it to speak to me and reveal what I need to know to work effectively at the deepest possible level. I may discover that the situation is not what I think it is or has more layers than I supposed.

Blending with the situation as it is rather than as how I think it is or should be is vital to my effectiveness as a world worker. I must suspend my own judgments, opinions, projections, and ideas and listen inwardly as I attune to a situation. Here is where allies can help or where the sacred can help, by lifting me out of my own limited perspective.

To truly listen, I may need to abandon for the moment even the idea of myself as a world worker or of any other role I may imagine myself as fulfilling, if that image projects its own unwanted information into the situation. If I think of myself as a hammer, I can project "nailness" into situations, for nails are what I work with. If I think of myself as a spiritual warrior for the light, then I can project darkness and evil into the situation, because that is what I want to fight. I need to get out of these more limited roles, at least at this initial stage. If in fact I discover the situation IS a nail, then I can happily go back to being a hammer; if I discover darkness or evil is truly present, I can go back to being a warrior for the Light. But first I must listen and see as clearly and unobstructedly as I can.

Having the space and focus to listen is part of the picture, and an important part. Another part is that in doing world work, we really are entering into another part of our being and taking on a different aspect of identity.

In effect we are making ourselves more open, more attuned, more engaged with subtle energies and forces than we may wish to be in the course of our normal activities. A surgeon may not wish to have at every moment of her daily life the same kind of fierce attention and concentration that she brings to her operating theater and her patient. Doing inner world work in a formal way IS entering into a heightened state or at least into a different state of consciousness than normal.

Who am I as a World Worker? Who are you? Not in a general everyday sense, but in the context of doing inner work?

I bring this up because my own training has always been that one engages with the inner cosmos with power. One stands in one's sovereignty and inner attunement with power. I may feel powerless in one or more areas of my everyday life, but in doing inner work, I need to stand in power, the power of the sacredness within me, the soul within me, the empersonal spirit within me, the power of my personhood and presence.

It is with this power that I link with allies and can create alliances; it is with this power that I hold an unobstructed channel open for the flow of sacredness. Think of the strength a fireman must have to hold a fire hose steady as many pounds of water pressure rush through it. Inner work doesn't require physical strength and power in the same way, but it does require a strength of integrity, character, identity, openness, and love to hold the firehouse of God.

Note that this is NOT a power of arrogance, of dominance, of will over anything or anyone. It is the power and joy of being oneself.

One of the ancillary benefits of doing World Work in this manner is that the felt sense of this power begins to enter our everyday lives as an inner confidence, a feeling of solidity and wholeness.

Notes & Reflections

Exercises for **World Work**

Exercise Nine:
Entering Stillness and Presence

This exercise is one I've adapted from an exercise taught by a friend of mine—and a most excellent spiritual teacher—R.J. Stewart, though in fact it is a very ancient exercise found in many spiritual traditions. R.J. Stewart uses it to enter into Stillness; I use it to enter into Stillness as well, but also into something else. Presence, perhaps?

Here it is. As always, if you feel at any time any discomfort, restlessness, or loss of attention in doing this exercise, just stop it and do something else that changes your attention and your energy in positive ways.

You can do this exercise standing if you wish, but you can also do it sitting. See what works best for you. Whether you are standing or sitting, however, imagine yourself standing.

Stretch out your arms and hands to your side in a comfortable manner, and spread out your legs and feet, again in a comfortable manner. The idea is that you are not standing with your limbs pressed together as if you were an exclamation point!

In this exercise, your legs and feet represent your connection with space, your arms and hands your connection with energy and activity, and your head your connection with time (after all, you can remember the past and imagine the future!).

In entering into Stillness and Presence, we are entering into a primal place beyond space, time, and energy or activity. It is the place from which space, time and energy emerge.

Imagine your arms and hands withdrawing into your torso until they disappear within you. You are withdrawing your awareness from its involvement with energy and activity.

Now imagine your head sinking into your shoulders and torso, until it disappears within you. You are withdrawing yourself from all sense of time.

Finally, imagine your legs and feet withdrawing up into your torso, disappearing inside of you. You do not fall but you float. You are withdrawing your engagement with space.

Now you are like an egg. You are in Stillness. There is no time, space or energy to disturb you. Just appreciate this state of Stillness.

In this Stillness, as in an egg, there is a presence of potential. There is a life that can emerge. It is filled with power, joy, anticipation, vitality, light. Feel that presence. Feel that potential. Feel the primal, pregnant stillness that surrounds you.

Now let that power and vitality, that potential and light, that paradox of stillness and activity, flow out from you as legs and feet. See your legs and feet extending from your torso back to the ground. You are once more extending yourself into Space.

Let that power and vitality, potential and light, stillness and activity, spirit and soul flow out from you as your head. Imagine your head emerging from between your shoulders, engaging you with Time.

Let that power and vitality, potential and light, stillness and activity, spirit and soul flow out from you as our arms and hands. Imagine your arms and hands extending once more out from your torso. You are engaging with the flow of energy in creation, the energy of doing and shaping.

Stand there feeling yourself pulsing with this presence and stillness, this power and vitality. If you are sitting down, stand up so that you may appreciate this more fully, letting your body physically reflect your inner stance.

Now move about a bit, feeling the energy, presence, and power move with you. Touch something, feeling this presence flow into whatever your touch, evoking a flow in response. Look at something and listen to something, feeling this presence active in your looking and hearing as these senses engage you with your world.

As you move on into your daily life from this exercise, feel the inner Stillness and presence moving with you.

You can do this exercise anywhere at anytime with practice, no matter what you are doing physically.

Notes & Reflections

Exercise Ten:
Being an Avatar

Important note: because of the world situation, I am going to cast this in terms of peace. But please feel free to substitute any other qualities or energies you may wish, depending on the nature of the world condition you wish to address.

Loosely defined, an Avatar is an embodiment of a sacred quality or presence. It is an act of mediation, bringing that quality or presence into accessibility and action in an environment in which it is not active, hard to access, invisible, or in some way not as apparent and available as it could be.

In this exercise, we are going to be Avatars of Peace (but see Important Note above for a qualification...).

This exercise has three steps. The first one is entirely inner; the second two are outwardly directed.

Step One

Sit quietly and enter into stillness using whatever method is comfortable and familiar to you. You may certainly use the exercise I have offered if you wish.

When you feel composed inwardly, enter your inner theater of the heart and mind, your place of imagination and imagery.

Imagine yourself in a place of spiritual power and initiation. This place is also resonant with feelings of honor, gifting, blessing, and empowerment. In this place, you are being honored. You are being initiated. You are being gifted. You are being blessed. You are being heightened and empowered in your spiritual capacity.

Please enter into the felt sense of this place. Feel in your body, in your mind and heart, just what it is like—what sensations are present— in this place of honoring, initiation, blessing, gifting, and empowerment, all directed upon you.

You know instinctively that you are worthy for whatever you receive, for whatever you feel.

A Presence enters this space with you. It is a Presence of the sacred quality of Peace. Pay attention to what this feels like to you. What is this Peace to you? How do you feel it in your body, your mind, your heart? What sensations, images, ideas, insights, feelings, arise in you in the presence of this quality of Divine Peace?

This Presence of Peace enters into and merges with you. You become an embodiment of it; you are an avatar of this Peace. It radiates within you; it radiates from you.

What does this feel like? What is the felt sense of being this Peace? This is most important to discern. What does it feel like in your body? Where do you feel it most in your body? What does it feel like in your mind or in your heart? What does it feel like spiritually? What sensations, images, ideas, feelings, insights, energies, or experiences arise in you as you accept being an Avatar of Peace?

The space you are in constantly supports you in taking this on. It reminds you over and over again: "You are loved. You are worthy. You have the power and the wisdom to embody this Peace." Let the empowering, gifting, blessing, initiating power of this space blend with the Presence of Peace within you, stabilizing it, grounding it, affirming it so there is no doubt, no question, no fear: you ARE a Presence, an Avatar, of Peace.

When you feel secure in this awareness, when you have a firm felt sense in your body, mind, and heart of what it means, what it is like, to be this Avatar of Peace (and remember, what it feels like is unique to you; someone else might feel it very differently. You might feel it as a calm, quiet presence, someone else might feel it as a bright, radiant light, and so on...), then you are ready to leave this place of initiation and empowerment.

In your imagination, go to wherever you feel the Presence of Peace is needed. Walk the countryside of Iraq, for instance, or the streets of Baghdad, or go anywhere you wish and be with anyone you wish at any time you wish where you feel you wish to bring Peace.

You are traveling exclusively upon the inner. Your imagination is your link to the actual situation and people. You are in a subtle body which does not have many of the limitations of your physical body. So you are not limited by time or distance. You can be as small or large as you wish. You can walk on air, walk through walls, radiate Peace from every part of yourself. There is no limitation upon you in this form or in

126

this imaginal realm.

But at all times keep your imagining anchored in, grounded in, connected to your felt sense of being a Presence of Peace. Otherwise you are just wishing, just indulging in fantasy. Your inner body is made up of this strong and concrete felt sense of being. It is the power of this felt sense that you bring into the midst of your images. Your images may be "imaginary," but your felt sense of being the Avatar of Peace is not. That is the reality you bring into the imaginal connections with real world conditions.

So go where you wish, do what you wish, see yourself as a powerful and irresistible presence moving through whatever landscape you wish and interacting with situations where you wish peace to emerge. But always keep in touch with your felt sense of being the Avatar of Peace.

If you imagine scenes of destruction, pain, suffering, anger, hatred, and the like, remember, you do NOT take these on into yourself. Instead, you hold and irradiate them with the power of Divine Peace. See these situations changing as you do so. See healing taking place, destruction erased, anger and fear comforted and held in compassion and peace. Do not try and impose your feelings or thoughts on anyone or any situation, but let the natural power of Peace free reign to act. Remember, you are on an imaginal realm, so if you imagine healing taking place, it is not something you are forcing but a suggestion to all levels of consciousness connected to that situation to be open to and aware of the possibilities of healing.

You are not MAKING something happen; you are illustrating what CAN happen and creating an energistic pathway upon the imaginal realm for it to happen in reality.

When you feel restless, or feel that felt sense of being the Avatar of Peace beginning to slip, or feel tired, then it is time to stop. There is no required duration for this exercise. Being an avatar of peace for ten seconds contributes greatly to the world, as much as being one for ten minutes. The issue is not how long you do it but the quality of presence you bring to the process. Ten seconds of a powerful presence is worth ten hours of diffused and unfocused imaginal wishing. Pay attention to your body and your mind and heart; they will generally tell you when you have had enough.

When you are done, return to the place of empowerment, gifting, honoring and just bask in its energy for a time. Reenter stillness. Let the Presence of Peace soak into your bones, as it were; let it bring you Peace and blessing.

Then focus your attention with grace and gratitude upon your body and upon your physical surroundings. Open your eyes and bring yourself wholly back into connection with your physical world.

This step of the exercise has ended.

I want to pause here to say something about doing imaginal work. An imaginal image can have power in its self, but it primarily acts as a link between one level and another. I may not know, for instance, just what is happening in Baghdad, but I can imagine what is happening in Baghdad. That imaginal image is a link between my consciousness (and any spiritual forces to which my consciousness is attuned) and the energy field of that city.

Will any image work? My imagination of Baghdad may be wildly off the mark. Does that matter?

What makes the link work is not necessarily the accuracy of the image but the power and reality of the felt sense I have of the spiritual force I wish to offer to that place. Without that felt sense, grounded in my body, I may well just be dealing with fantasy and images disconnected with any reality. I need to feel both the spiritual qualities and energies I wish to contribute in my body, heart, and mind, and I also need to feel myself physically in Baghdad, even if my imaginal image is off the mark.

Suppose I were blind and deaf. How would I experience Baghdad, or any other city? I would have to experience it in my imagination, supported by whatever senses I can call upon. Any research I do to give me a real feeling for what being in Baghdad physically would be like will help make my images more powerful and grounding. But the real power in the work does not come from the imaginative image but from the power and reality of my felt sense of the energy or quality I am embodying and of the work I am doing. The image needs to be held and supported or nourished by this felt sense.

If I imagine myself walking through the streets of Baghdad, let's say, with streamers of light, healing, compassion, and peace radiating out from my extremities and with my body luminescent with the glow of spirit and if I imagine that whomever I meet or see, whether Iraqi or American, soldier or civilian, is embraced in that Light such that they immediately become healed, peaceful, and filled with a sense of love and safety, this is an imaginal narrative. Is it really happening? Probably not in that way. But what happens in the imaginal becomes a template for what can happen in the physical. It is not a one-to-one correspondence necessarily, but it is a suggestive and energistic correspondence. It sets energies in motion to fulfill the essence of that image, if not necessarily its form. I am picturing miraculous healing, for instance, but the effect of this is to shape and incline energies already present there towards healing or having a healing effect or opening the way for people to find the healing they need.

In that sense it's like projecting a movie; the actual action in the movie may not be replicated in physical life but it can inspire equivalent qualities and energies to arise in the audience which will lead to some form of manifestation on the physical. Watching Rocky, for instance, won't turn me into a boxer, but it may make it easier for me to attune to, embody and express qualities of determination and courage.

The power, conviction, and compellingness within the images I create may help empower the link, but I need to keep grounded in the actual quality of what I want to transmit. If I get caught up in or lost in the images, that link can actually be broken as I go spinning off, so to speak, in realms of fantasy. But if the felt sense, the grounded sense in my body, mind and heart of the qualities with which I am working, is maintained with clarity, then the images I use will come to reflect the power of that felt sense and will be a powerful link with the actual physical reality of what is going on.

Step Two

You should do this exercise in a place where you can be alone and undisturbed. It is primarily an indoor exercise, but you can do it outdoors if you can be in a secluded area. You will want to maintain stillness and focus as you do this exercise, and this may be difficult if you are also needing to engage with people. You will, however, be active and walking around physically, so choose your location accordingly.

In this exercise, repeat Step One up to the point at which you have a felt sense of being an Avatar of Peace (or whatever quality you have chosen). Go to the empowering, gifting, blessing place, tune into the presence of the quality you choose—which in this example is Peace—and merge with it.

This time, however, do not take an imaginal journey. Just sit for a moment and feel the felt sense of this presence in your body, in your heart, and in your mind. Feel it in your hands and feet, your fingers and toes.

Open your eyes. Get up from your chair and walk about your house or wherever you are. Go about your normal affairs, but maintain as long as you can a sense of being the Avatar of Peace. Let peace flow from your hands into everything you touch. Let peace flow from your feet into the floor or ground wherever you walk. Let peace flow from your eyes towards all that you see. Let peace flow from your ears to embrace whatever you hear. Let peace surround you and as it surrounds you, let it flow out to surround everything around you.

In this Step Two, I suggest you not engage with people. In this exercise, you are practicing maintaining your felt sense of the spiritual power of peace (or whatever quality you have chosen) while being active in the midst of a physical environment. If you find yourself losing this felt sense, just pause and reattune in stillness to this quality.

The idea is to feel the interactive nature of this quality as you radiate it into your environment and receive the response from that environment. Be aware of any sensations you may feel, any thoughts, feelings, insights, and the like. Be aware of when you begin to lose the felt sense of peace and what is happening at that moment. Be aware of how difficult or easy it is to maintain it.

Who do you feel like in this situation? Does it feel natural? Organic? If so, why? If not, why not?

When you feel tired or feel the energy and felt sense of peace has diminished and it is hard for you to hold it, sit down. Take a moment to reenter stillness. Go back to the place of grace, of gifting, blessing and empowerment. Sit in that energy and presence for a time. Then focus your attention with grace and gratitude upon your body and upon your physical surroundings. Open your eyes and bring yourself wholly back into connection with your physical world.

This step of the exercise has ended.

Step Three

In this exercise, repeat Steps One and Two up to the point at which you have a felt sense of being an Avatar of Peace (or whatever quality you have chosen). Go to the empowering, gifting, blessing place, tune into the presence of the quality you choose—which in this example is Peace—and merge with it.

This time, however, do not take an imaginal journey. Just sit for a moment and feel the felt sense of this presence in your body, in your heart, and in your mind. Feel it in your hands and feet, your fingers and toes.

Open your eyes. Get up from your chair and go about your normal affairs, but maintain as long as you can a sense of being the Avatar of Peace. Let peace flow from your hands into everything you touch. Let peace flow from your feet into the floor or ground wherever you walk. Let peace flow from your eyes towards all that you see. Let peace flow from your ears to embrace whatever you hear. Let peace surround you and as it surrounds you, let it flow out to surround everything around you.

Unlike Step Two, this time I suggest you do engage with people as normal. In this exercise, you are practicing maintaining your felt sense of the spiritual power of peace (or whatever quality you have chosen) while being active in your everyday environment. If you find yourself losing this felt sense, just pause and re-attune in stillness to this quality.

The idea is to feel the interactive nature of this quality as you radiate it into your environment and receive the response from that environment. Be aware of any sensations you may feel, any thoughts, feelings, insights, and the like. Be aware of when you begin to lose the felt sense of peace and what is happening at that moment. Be aware of how difficult or easy it is to maintain it.

In dealing with people, can you radiate this felt sense of peace (or whatever quality you are working with) to them? Can you interact with them normally and still maintain the sense of being enfolded in the quality you have chosen and able to radiate it? Just be aware of how difficult or easy this may be, of their reactions, and of any way in which the flow of this radiant quality may increase or decrease as you go about your normal routines with people.

Who do you feel like in this situation? Does it feel natural? Organic? If so, why? If not, why not?

It is important in this exercise that you not draw attention to yourself in any extraordinary or unusual way. You are ideally working towards a capacity to hold and carry, and radiate, a spiritual energy as a natural and organic way of being, an ordinary way of being that nevertheless blesses your environment and all within it.

When you feel tired or feel the energy and felt sense of peace has diminished and it is hard for you to hold it, sit down. Take a moment to reenter stillness. Go back to the place of grace, of gifting, blessing and empowerment. Sit in that energy and presence for a time. Then focus your attention with grace and gratitude upon your body and upon your physical surroundings. Open your eyes and bring yourself wholly back into connection with your physical world.

This step of the exercise has ended.

Notes & Reflections

Exercise Eleven:
Loving Hands

This is a basic exercise.

In this exercise you begin by putting yourself into as loving a mood as possible, centering that love in your heart.

You might do this by remembering or imagining people and places that you love. Allow that love to fill your heart until it becomes a flame ablaze with a compassionate and loving fire. If you wish, connect with spirit and the Sacred and allow their holy love and All-Compassion to join with yours, turning your heart into a flaming sun of love.

From your heart, imagine this love flowing throughout your body, coursing down rivers of blood, lymph, and nerve. Specifically, see it flowing into you hands, pooling in your palms, flowing into your fingers where this love strains to leap out and flow into the world.

Now imagine your hands filled with strength, tenderness, grace, and gentleness, as if you are about to touch and hold something that is very precious and very loved by you. Sense your fingers as messengers of your heart's love, of the holy love flowing throughout you.

As you center this felt sense of love and blessing and power in your hands, fed by the connection with your heart and by your heart's connection with the sacred, just touch something. Feel the love flowing from your fingers around whatever it is you are touching. Your fingers are making this love available, but not forcing it in any way upon whatever you are touching. You are not imposing. You are offering. And if this offer is accepted, the love will flow from you into whatever you are touching, blessing it and turning it into a resource of love as well from which this love can flow out into the world.

You can turn your hands into loving hands - pools of love, blessing, empowerment, and even healing - anytime you wish, anywhere you wish, with anyone or anything you wish. The key is that you are not forcing or imposing anything but simply offering and making available an energy of love flowing from your hands. Your task is to provide the loving hands; it is up to the other whether to accept it.

Notes & Reflections

Exercise Twelve
Midas Touch of Peace

Imagine that everything and everyone in the world is connected by invisible threads of energy, so that whatever you touch—whether it's a person, a book, a table, a cat, or a dirty dish you are washing in the sink—puts you in touch as well with everything and everyone else.

Second, imagine that you are like the mythic King Midas, except that instead of turning everything you touch to gold, you turn it to peacefulness and wellbeing. To do this, draw to mind whatever images you may have of what peace means to you and feel the quality of peace in your mind and body. For that one moment, step into peace. Then concentrate that felt sense of what peace means to you, out from your heart, down your arms and into your hands. Feel the spirit of peace in your hands and fingers, so that they glow and tingle with peace.

Third, touch something. It could be anything. What it is doesn't matter at the moment, for we are imagining that everything is connected to everything else (which is what both scientists and mystics tell us is the nature of reality anyway). When you do, feel the radiance and power of peace in your hands flow around whatever you are touching, inviting it to receive this peace. This peace can easily flow into whatever you are touching if it is open to it; if it is not, it simply surrounds it like a radiant cloud and makes itself available should it be wanted or needed.

This exercise can have a special power when you touch another person mindfully and with caring with the "Midas Touch of Peace." People will feel it, and you will, too. It is hard to engage in conflict when you are touching someone in a spirit of peace.

Once you have a sense of this flow of peace, then try it with your tongue so that you can only speak words that carry the energy of peace. Instead of the gift of gab, give your tongue the gift of peace. It's hard to speak words of violence and conflict when you're feeling your tongue glowing with peace!

Try this exercise with your eyes. Let peace fill your eyes and then flow to whatever and whomever you are looking upon. Instead of x-ray vision like Superman, you have the Super Gaze of Peace. It's hard to see another as an enemy when you are looking upon them with peace.

Put peace into your feet and walk peace into the earth.

Put peace into your heart, and let your life be a heart that circulates peace throughout your environment.

Remember that at the heart of peace are love and a caring for the wellbeing of another. Practice putting love into your hands, your eyes, your tongue, and your feet as well.

Notes & Reflections

_____

_____

_____

_____

_____

_____

_____

_____

_____

_____

_____

_____

_____

_____

_____

_____

_____

_____

Exercise Thirteen:
Massaging the World

This exercise builds on the Loving Hands practice.

In thinking about what you are doing here, imagine that you are a body worker about to give a massage. The actual pain that the client is experiencing is deep within the body, out of reach and beyond your ability to reach it directly. But by working with the muscles and tissues that are available to you, you set a relaxing, healing force to work within the body as a whole.

This exercise operates on the premise that like the body, the world is a whole system in which every part is connected to every other part. By working on one layer, deeper layers can be affected in positive ways. By working on what is at hand, conditions that are distant can be affected as well, particularly if those distant or deeper areas are held in mind and the connections affirmed.

Begin by doing the Loving Hands exercise.

As you feel the love pooling and radiating in your hands, ask that this love become a force for healing and restoration.

Put your hands on something in your environment that is touching a floor or the earth. If you can put your hand on the earth directly this is preferable, but it is not necessary. Just visualize the connections that exist between whatever you are touching and the earth as a whole. [NOTE: For this exercise, it may be better not to use something that you can hold; whatever you touch should have a physical connection to the earth, if only through a floor. However, if you have a strong sense of visualization and can feel the connections existing between an object and the earth, then you can use anything you wish.]

If you wish, let your fingers move upon whatever you are touching, just as if you were massaging it. You want to feel fingers of energy and love moving deeper to touch and massage the energetic field of whatever you are touching. As you do, let your attention be upon letting your energy serve and bless the energy and presence of whatever you are touching and through it, the larger energy field of your immediate environment. Allow yourself to come into a loving and blessing connection with the energy field or fields of your immediate environment. At this stage, you are not trying to do anything more than bless and "massage" the energy that is around you, the world you immediately inhabit.

As you feel a state of integration and harmony and flow develop between you and your environment, call to mind a situation in the world that you would like to serve and to which you wish to offer an energy of love, healing, peace, and blessing. Continue to extend a healing, calming, blessing energy into your environment, but now imagine the lines of connection between where you are and the distant place you wish to bless. Don't try to "go" there in your imagination. Keep yourself focused on blessing and serving what you can immediately touch, the environment around you. But just know that through the medium of a deeper Intelligence within the body of the earth, your intent to heal and bless will be received and honored in places where it is needed but which you cannot reach directly in any physical way.

When you feel tired or restless or have a sense of completion, just remove your hands. Sit for a moment and let the energy of love and spirit circulate through your body, relaxing and empowering you and filling you with grace. Then give thanks, and go about your daily affairs.

Notes & Reflections

Exercise Fourteen:
Attuning to the Earth Star

This is a simple imaginal exercise.

Imagine at the heart of the earth shines a star. This star is green and radiates an energy of life. This radiance is empowering, life-giving, and nourishing. It fosters growth and unfoldment, balance and wholeness.

This star is the light within the earth; it is the presence of the Planetary Being for whom this world is its outermost form. The light of this star is the radiance of its intelligence, wisdom, and love.

Imagine this star rising up from the earth beneath you and engulfing you so that you are embraced and surrounded by its radiant light. You are within this green star, this earth-light. Feel its presence permeating you. What is this like? What is your felt sense of being in attunement to this Earth Star? How do you feel? What images, sensations, ideas, feelings arise for you?

Just feel yourself held and uplifted within this Earth Star. Part of you is one with the earth anyway, so the light of this Star is the light of home, a place where you belong, a place that nourishes and cherishes you.

Feel your own inner Earth Star awaken. Feel your analog, your equivalent to this Earth Light awakening and radiating within you. Feel yourself as a source of life-supporting, life-empower energy. Feel yourself empowered by the Earth Star to be a star of empowerment for others. What is this like?

Imagine the radiance of this Earth Star and your own unique earth light bathing your immediate environment with its presence.

Just be in the presence of this radiant Earth Star for as long as you wish. Then let it return into the earth. See it sinking back into the core of the planet. But as it does, your own inner Earth Star remains bright and radiant. Pay attention to the felt sense of being an Earth Star yourself.

Whenever you need to attune to the Planetary Being and its radiance, return to this image of the Earth Star in the world beneath and around you, and within your own being as well.

Notes & Reflections

Exercise Fifteen:
Invoking Aid from the Earth Logos
(or planetary being)

In doing World Work, there are many times when you may not or should not act on your own. It is good in any kind of spiritual work to have a buddy to work with, but this is not always possible. But having a spiritual ally can be very important, too.

You always have the option (and it is often a good idea) to invoke the presence of the Sacred as you do World Work or of any inner ally who is important to you as a symbol of helpfulness, compassion, healing, love, power, and protection. A Christian, for instance, would most likely invoke and ask for the presence of the Christ.

In this exercise, you are invoking the aid and assistance of the Planetary Being, called in esoteric literature the Earth Logos. All that happens anywhere upon the earth to any creature or human upon the earth or to any environment upon the earth happens within the presence and life of this being. We are all held in its compassion and love, and of course its power. So it is a good ally to have, a good presence to serve with our contribution and love, and a good source of guidance in our World Work.

This exercise builds on the previous one, Attuning to the Earth Star, However, you should always feel free to attune to this being in anyway that feels right and comfortable to you. The important thing is attuning to the felt sense of your relationship with the presence of this Planetary Intelligence and Life.

Do the exercise "Attuning to the Earth Star".

When you feel yourself embraced by and within the Earth Star, pay attention to the source from which this Star itself is emanating. In a manner of speaking, this Star is the aura or field of a great Planetary Being. At the heart of this Star is this Being, aware of you, waiting for your attention in return.

As a child of earth, you are always worthy to be with this Planetary Being and to co-create and participate with it in serving the wellbeing of the earth. You are always welcome in its presence.

You can imagine this presence anyway you wish. You might, for example, see it as a human–like presence of either gender (or no gender) standing in light at the heart of this Star, or it might just be a presence of light. Or it might take the form of a tree or an animal or of the planet itself. It will enter your imagination and commune with you in any way you wish or that is appropriate. It will always be more than any form you can imagine anyway.

Approach this Being with love, sharing its desire to serve and bless the world you both inhabit. Approach in strength and with a sense of your power as an incarnate Self, able to meet and co-create with its power as the Soul and Spirit of this planet.

Once you feel a felt sense in your body and psyche of being in the presence of this Being and in relationship with it, state what it is you wish to do in your world work. Ask it for its assistance and blessing, and for its guidance. Also offer your own participation and service in ways that it may think best or in answer to a need it may present. In effect, you are allies, two partners seeking to help each other. Be silent and listen. Be open to any intuition, images, thoughts, feelings or wisdom that may arise. It will never tell you what to do, but it will make suggestions. It will never infringe upon your sovereignty or integrity, nor ask for your help in ways that are beyond you.

If you have a specific World Work in mind, a specific task you have set yourself, a specific situation you wish to help anywhere in the world, then name that situation, announce your intent, and ask for the help of this Planetary Being as your ally. If you have nothing specific in mind, then ask for its suggestions for how you may be of service.

Pay attention to the felt sense in your body of being in attunement and connection with this Being. It is this to this felt sense that you will return in memory when you wish to renew this contact. It is this felt sense, and the power it brings, that you wish to carry with you into your World Work.

Once you feel aligned with and in harmonious integrity and connection with the Planetary Being at the heart of the Earth Star, go forth and do whatever World Work it is your intention to do or which you choose to do in honor of any suggestions you may have received from this Planetary Being.

As always, when you feel tired, restless, a diminished energy, or a sense that your inner work is complete, then stop your World Work. Go to an inner place of quiet, of rest, of peace and grace, beauty and harmony. Allow it to fill your being, your body, mind, heart, and soul, restoring you to harmony with your everyday life.

Give thanks to your ally, the Planetary Being, for its energy, its presence, its wisdom, and for any help or gifts you feel you have received from it. See yourself disengaging from the Earth Star and from the intense working relationship you may have co-created, though you can certainly carry a sense of this presence with you into your daily life. Refocus your attention with grace and balance back into your everyday life and your ordinary, personal affairs.

These exercises are only a small sample of ways you can do World Work using your imagination, your attunement and attention, your love and your will. They really only scratch the surface, but hopefully they are helpful in pointing out a direction in which to go in your work.

As a world worker, you ultimately need to find ways that work for you. For one person it might be prayer, for another ritual, for another imaginal, magical exercises such as I have offered. Ideally, your world work becomes an overflow from your own everyday presence of attunement to love and to the earth in the context of your ordinary life. Potentially, there is never a time when you are not doing World Work in the sense of influencing the environment with your thoughts, feelings, and actions.

So be bold! Experiment, explore, and learn the ways that work best to attune you to your own inner light and strength, to the light of spiritual allies and of the earth itself, and to situations of need or of possibility upon the world. Always be sure to buffer yourself and to be a buffer for others. There is already too much fear, too much anger, too much frustration in the world for you to pass it on to others.

Discover who you are as a World Worker. Both you and our planet will be the better for it.

Blessings!

Notes & Reflections

What's Next?

We hope that you enjoyed and benefited from what you have engaged so far. Though designed to be complete in itself, this Textbook is also part of a larger developing program. There is much more to Incarnational Spirituality overall.

The Lorian Association through the Lorian center for Incarnational Spirituality offers a variety of mechanisms to support the practices suggested by this book.

In addition, Incarnational Spirituality is an evolving study. We encourage you to explore and experiment and, if you wish, to share what you discover with the larger Lorian community. In this way, Incarnational Spirituality can grow and benefit from the ongoing experience and insights of all of us who wish to see the world benefit from its contributions.

If you wish to proceed, what's next? We have tried to provide several options so you can interact with the material in a variety of ways depending on your life situation. Here are some of those options:

1. View, listen to, or read any of the DVD's, audio CD's, website articles, and booklets available free and through the web from Lorian.

2. Sign up for Lorian's free e-newsletter and/or David Spangler's periodic e-articles. Simply go to www.lorian.org and click on the newsletter sign up button on the home page. And, while you're there browse through some of the other articles, information and links on our website. If you are on our mailing list, you will receive every two weeks an article from David Spangler called "David's Desk," a monthly e-newsletter, and announcements about special activities and classes.

3. Engage in a program of self directed learning using material produced by the Lorian Center for Incarnational Spirituality (shown below).

4. You may also wish to connect with a group in your area studying Lorian material or form a study group yourself. Lorian is available to supply materials and support. Besides this textbook these include:

Incarnational Spirituality: *A strategy to bless our World* An introduction to Incarnational Spirituality by David Spangler $15.

Embodying Eden: Roots of a New Culture A workbook on Loving Self, Others, World, and Actions by Jeremy Berg $15.

Manifestation: Creating the life you love – Card Deck and Manual by David Spangler $25. This book and deck can also be purchased with four audio CD's covering an introductory talk and one day workshop on Manifestation by David for $55.

The Starshaman Home Mystery School™ Series by David Spangler. These Four Modules cover the foundations of Incarnational Spirituality in depth and include original textbooks extracted from David's three month online classes of the same name. Each module is unique but all include Audio CD's of workshops augmenting the class text. Other materials such as Incarnation card decks, the Incarnational Mandala, talismanic materials, audio/visual aids, and other items in support of the text and exercises are also provided in the packages. The modules are:

- **Home-Crafting: Self, Sacred and Blessing**
- **Space-Crafting: The Incarnational Self**
- **Crafting Inner Alliances: Working with Spiritual Forces**
- **World-Crafting: Manifestation and Service**

These Starshaman modules are complete in themselves as a comprehensive training. And, they can be used as the foundation for further development in World Service and other spiritual work. Each module includes two weeks online live with David Spangler. You may also engage these modules interactively with David Spangler online for two months as a systematic training. Additional fees apply. Please check the website for pricing, availability, and class schedules.

5. Sponsor a Lorian workshop or talk in your area. Please contact Lorian for availability and arrangements.

6. Participate in Soul Friending. Our website lists several trained Spiritual Directors/Soul Friends associated with Lorian. They work with clients in person and by phone to deepen into their experience of the sacred, develop their spiritual practice, and work through personal spiritual blocks and opportunities.

7. Participate in Soul Friending. We can recommend several trained Spiritual Directors/Soul Friends associated with Lorian. They work with clients in person and by phone to deepen into their experience of the sacred, develop their spiritual practice, and work through personal spiritual blocks and opportunities.

8. Lorian also offers advanced training and longer-term programs for those who both wish them and qualify. Such programs can lead to certifications or a Masters Degree in Contemporary Spirituality (MCS).

9. Participate in the Lorian Associates. This world wide group makes up our growing community of people engaged with applying Incarnational Spirituality in their lives and sharing the results with each other. The only requirement for participation is to a working knowledge and practice of Incarnational Spirituality.

About the Publisher

Lorian Press is a private, for profit business which publishes works approved by the Lorian Association. Current titles from David Spangler and others can be found on the Lorian website www.lorian.org, at www.davidspangler.com, and at www.lorianpress.com.

The Lorian Association is a not-for-profit educational organization. Its work is to help people bring the joy, healing, and blessing of their personal spirituality into their everyday lives. This spirituality unfolds out of their unique lives and relationships to Spirit, by whatever name or in whatever form that Spirit is recognized.

For more information, go to www.lorian.org, email info@lorian.org, or write to:

The Lorian Association
P.O. Box 1368
Issaquah, WA 98027